BISCUITS ACROSS THE BRAZOS

BISCUITS ACROSS
THE BRAZOS

Jim H. Ainsworth

SUNSTONE
PRESS

Sunstone books may be purchased for educational, business, or sales promotional use. For information please write: Special Markets Department, Sunstone Press, P.O. Box 2321, Santa Fe, New Mexico 87504-2321.

Printed on acid free paper

———————————————————————————

Library of Congress Cataloging-in-Publication Data

Ainsworth, Jim H.
  Biscuits across the Brazos : a recollection of a memorable horseback and wagon journey / by Jim H. Ainsworth.
      p. cm.
  Originally published: Campbell, Tex. : Season of Harvest Publications, c2000.
  ISBN 978-0-86534-754-0 (softcover : alk. paper)
  1. Brazos River Region (Tex.)--Description and travel. 2. Brazos River Region (Tex.)--History, Local. 3. Ainsworth, Jim H.--Travel--Texas--Brazos River Region. 4. Ainsworth, Jim H.--Family. 5. Packhorse camping--Texas--Brazos River Region. 6. Trail riding--Texas--Brazos River Region. 7. Wagon trains--Texas--Brazos River Region. I. Title.
  F392.B842A35 2010
  976.4--dc22

                                        2009049904

———————————————————————————

Published in

WWW.SUNSTONEPRESS.COM
SUNSTONE PRESS / POST OFFICE BOX 2321 / SANTA FE, NM 87504-2321 /USA
(505) 988-4418 / ORDERS ONLY (800) 243-5644 / FAX (505) 988-1025

Dedicated to the memories of Arch and Teadon Ainsworth
and to the Texas folklore and family history they loved.
Thanks for passing it on.

Contents

Foreword

I never met Jim Ainsworth, but I know him fairly well after reading of his duplication in 1998 of the journey of his great-grandparents in 1918 from Baird, in Callahan County, to their new home in Delta County. I know that he loves Texas history, his family—ancestors, siblings, and descendants—and that he is a "dreamer" and a "do-er."

Some things are peculiar about that first journey of Hiram Griffin Ainsworth, his wife, Eva Catherine Lowe Ainsworth, and their five children, Mable, Ola, Arch, Richard (Teadon), and Exle. One thing was their direction: instead of the more familiar westering impulse, the Ainsworth's headed east to get to more rain, good soil, and trees. For another, this happened in 1918, long after the frontier line had found the Pacific Ocean.

The Ainsworths were pioneer people anyway. Having worked for the Texas & Pacific Railroad as an engineer, Hiram knew an easier way to travel. Instead, the family made their way to East Texas in a covered wagon with only two horses and one tied along side. And they passed on their spirit to grandsons Jim and Marion Ainsworth, who decided to replicate their grandparent's odyssey in 1998.

Jim's motivation for organizing the trip was rooted in a horseback trip to Wyoming, two biscuits preserved in a jar, and a phone call from cousin Marion. The western ride reminded him of the hardships his grandparents had endured to relocate to East Texas; the biscuits had been given to his father, Teadon, by a favorite Aunt Minnie when he left Callahan County; Teadon had denied himself the pleasure of eating the biscuits to preserve the memory of Aunt Minnie and what had been left behind.

Jim determined to retrace their steps, to experience, as much as the passage of eighty years permitted, what they had experienced. Marion and Jim had no trouble convincing each other to go, and friend Charles Horchem was determined to accompany them. Several others participated for part of the trip.

The riders made some concessions to modernity—a truck and trailer for scouting camp sites, cameras, and so forth, but as nearly as they could they recreated, as a way of preserving, the original journey of the Ainsworths on horse back and covered wagon. The first group sought a new home; for the the second group, it was a way of coming home.

Along the way Jim, Marion, Charles, and the others found a wealth of new friends who took in traveling strangers the way folks once did, elevating simple hospitality into grace. Their hosts shared the journey across Texas and back in time.

Jim made sure that every family member got a chance to participate, regardless of age, so they would remember the old ways. He admits that many wondered "why" when they heard of his plan and that once it was completed, they may have asked "so what?" But I know why he did it.

Jim says that even if one person reads of the trip and says they wish they could have been there, if one grandchild (one might have to be a grandparent to understand this) says "Look what Papa did," the enterprise would be justified. True enough, but there is more.

Jim was looking for himself. A journey that began at the grave of one ancestor and ended near the resting place of a child of the original trip teaches more than can be imagined about continuity of family and what lies within oneself. As Jim says, "What a man has experienced, no power on earth can take away." The deed is in the doing, and Jim Ainsworth is a doer.

I remember a line from a seafaring novel read half a century ago concerning one who had not traveled, had not experienced much. The novelist mentioned a fellow's backside, and called it the watermark of his sails. I can only imagine the condition of Jim's backside after fourteen days in the saddle, but I know his heart was happy.

Archie P. McDonald
Executive Director/Editor
East Texas Historical Association
Regents Professor
Stephen F. Austin State University
Nacogdoches, Texas

Acknowledgments

Thanks to Dr. Fred Tarpley for his invaluable assistance in editing and for his thoughtful suggestions on everything to do with this work. Also, thanks to Dr. James Conrad for his insight and patience with my many questions as well as assistance with photography and other wise counsel. My sincere appreciation to Copeland Tinney for his photographic art that made it possible to capture two old biscuits in a jar that had not been opened in eighty-two years.

To my trail riding buddies, thanks for making it a memorable experience that inspired me to write this narrative.

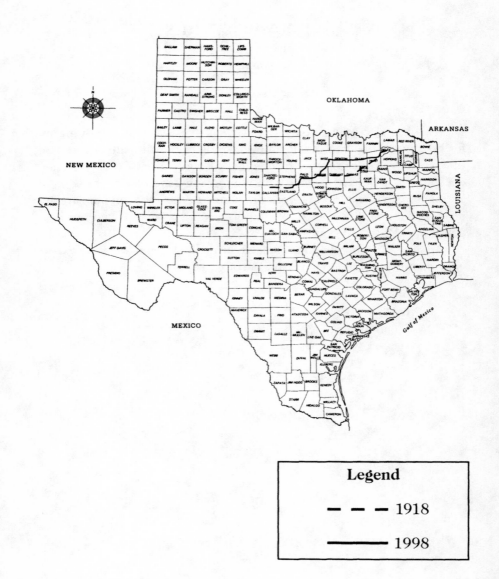

Introduction

This story is about two family journeys across Texas. Both journeys were by covered wagons and horses. Both covered an approximate distance of 325 miles in fourteen days. The first took place in 1918—the second in 1998. Travelers on the first journey included Hiram Griffin Ainsworth (1879-1962), his wife Eva Catherine Lowe Ainsworth (1881-1939) and their five children—Mabel (age fourteen), Ola (age twelve), Arch (age nine), Richard (Teadon) (age seven), and Exle (age two). They made the journey in search of a better life. Hiram had been an engineer for the Texas & Pacific Railroad, but wanted to work for himself as a farmer and rancher. Conditions around Baird and Ranger in Central West Texas were harsh with sparse rainfall. To farm or ranch successfully required a lot of land. Stories from his brother Rance had attracted him to the ample rainfall, fertile black soil, and large oak trees in Northeast Texas. He made a courageous decision to take his family east with only a covered wagon pulled by two horses with one young colt riding along side. Imagine the gravity of that decision. He left a well-paying job to travel across a country with five small children and a hand drawn map .

The second journey took place eighty years later with the sons of Arch and Teadon—Marion (Shep) Ainsworth (age fifty-seven) and Jim Ainsworth (age fifty-three)—trying to recreate both the circumstances and the spirit of their ancestors' trip. They were joined on the trip by Charles Horchem as cook and wagon driver and Jordan Brown as assistant cocinero. Jerald Thomas, a close friend, was also along for a major part of the trip. Other family members joined the wagon and horsemen at various times so that the whole family could be part of the adventure. This is their story.

BISCUITS ACROSS THE BRAZOS

Jim H. Ainsworth

Aunt Minnie (left) and Eva Ainsworth

Fall 1918

‹~‹~~~›~›

Aunt Minnie's Biscuits

The seven-year-old boy was making his usual morning trip to Aunt Minnie's for hot buttered biscuits. His dark skin and almost black eyes contrasted sharply with his blond hair. Although signs of fall were in the air, the morning was still warm. Dressed in his standard overalls, his bare calloused feet kicked up dust from the lingering dry weather typical of West Texas. He had left his brogan shoes in the wagon for use only when needed. Teadon always looked forward to going to Aunt Minnie's. Aunt Minnie was both an aunt and a grandmother. She was older than his mother and had served as both mother and sister to her. Teadon loved her biscuits and he loved her. Her house was just a short run along the banks of the Leon River through mesquites and scrub oaks. This morning's trip was different, however. Today, his entire family would be leaving their home in West Texas for good.

As he got his usual hug from Aunt Minnie, his family arrived in their covered wagon. He was excited about the journey, but the finality of his visit with Minnie hadn't hit him until she gave him a second hug and two extra biscuits. Her admonition in a breaking voice, "Don't forget me," made tears well up in his eyes that he didn't quite understand. Minnie hugged all the children and gave each two of her special buttered biscuits wrapped in wax paper. With tearful goodbyes to sister Eva Catherine and her family complete, she shielded her eyes from the rising sun as she watched the wagon head east.

Hiram Griffin Ainsworth had spent most of his adult life as an employee

3

of the Texas and Pacific Railroad. The pay and work were both reasonable and he had advanced to engineer, but brother Rance had left earlier for Northeast Texas. He had written about the ample rainfall, fertile black land, and big oak trees in Delta County. At thirty-nine, Hiram wanted to farm and possibly raise and train a few good horses. Mostly, he just wanted to work for himself. So Minnie tearfully watched her sister, her husband, and their five children leave on a journey that Hiram and Rance had estimated at over 325 miles. If they could average just over twenty miles per day, they should be there in just about sixteen days. Not exactly a trip that rivaled those earlier wagon trains that traveled across half of the United States, but it was going to be a challenging journey for a family traveling alone with five small children, no maps, not many roads, and no guide.

Hiram Ainsworth had marked his two sons and one daughter with the rust complexion, angular face and almost black eyes that verified his Native American ancestry. Eva had beautiful olive skin and a mischievous smile. She passed on those features to two of her three daughters. Both parents were excited but apprehensive about their journey. The Ainsworths carried only one extra horse, Prince, a young colt not yet broken. He was tied to the harness next to his mother. Thinking he would stay with his mother, Hiram released him for a few minutes to unharness the two horses pulling the wagon. Prince did not hesitate to leave his mother and return home in a fast trot. Hiram had to saddle the colt's mother and return the entire distance overnight to retrieve him. Retelling the story years later, Hiram said that he would have let the colt go, but he knew what a fine horse he would become.

Teadon was a nickname that had begun when brother Arch tried to pronounce his real name, Richard Adolph. Along with older brother Archibald Marion (age nine), Teadon was joined in the wagon by older sisters Mabel (age fourteen), Ola (age twelve) and younger sister Minnie Exle (age two). Teadon was still too excited about the trip to even be hungry at dinnertime, and Eva cooked a fine supper the first night over an open campfire. Next morning, however, his thoughts turned to Aunt Minnie's biscuits. He looked at them and thought of Aunt Minnie. As the other children eagerly enjoyed the last of their biscuits, Teadon just sat and looked at his. Though only twenty miles from home, he felt a thousand miles away from Aunt Minnie. He decided to keep her biscuits a while longer.

Teadon kept those biscuits until his death fifty-one years later. It's been eighty years now, and I still have Daddy's biscuits. I didn't appreciate how much they meant to him during his lifetime, although he told me the story of their wagon trip many times. As I reached my forties, family lore and history began to take on more meaning and interest. I often sat and looked at the biscuits—still sitting in a jar, the wax paper lying in wilted folds.

Arch (left) and Teadon Ainsworth

In 1994, I took a week-long horse-back ride in the Gros Ventre mountains in Wyoming to celebrate my fiftieth birthday. I thought a lot about my dad's journey during that adventure. I am sure that the "roughing it" I endured during that trip was nothing compared to the hardships that his family suffered. Two years later Marion Shepherd Ainsworth, Arch's son, called me at home one evening. Since Arch and Teadon had married sisters Nadelle and Hildred Alexander, Marion and I were double cousins. He said, "Let's ride horseback on the same trail that our dads took in 1918." After mentioning that Marion did not own a horse at the time, I asked, "How soon can you go?"

Hiram and Eva Ainsworth, 1942

June 1997 to May 1998

⟨ ornament ⟩

Planning the Trip

It took us over a year to get our business and personal lives organized enough to commit to the trip. During that time, the planned trip had evolved from just Marion and I riding horseback from Delta County in Northeast Texas to Baird in Callahan County. Old friend Charles Horchem, when hearing of the journey, made the flat and immediate statement, "I'm going." Charles, besides being a top notch chuck wagon cocinero, owned a fine Studebaker covered wagon circa 1890's. His wagon resembled the wagon that our parents traveled in. Also, he is a colorful and entertaining character. Besides that, we couldn't have kept him from going if we had wanted to. Our only problem now was finding something to pull the wagon. Another good friend, Jerald Thomas, provided the connection we needed. He knew of a fellow who had mules for loan or rent.

We visited Clyde Todd in Van, Texas and worked out an agreement to borrow his matched white mules. The mules had not been worked in a long time. When we got them caught and haltered, one tried to leave with Marion in tow. He lost his hat, but dug in his heels and held on until the mule gave up pulling him across the pasture. We now had a good-looking team to pull the wagon. With Charles and the mules along, we decided it would be more realistic and practical to leave from the same place our forebears had instead of reversing the trip.

Calvin and Jean Ainsworth, our cousins from Ranger, had asked if we could schedule a stop at the Ranger Annual Old Time Country Festival. Calvin and his wife Jean were well versed in Ainsworth history and lore and an integral part of our plans. We decided that the only way to make it work was to leave from Lake Leon near Ranger instead of from Baird as our parents had. That seemed suitable since our great-grandfather is buried in an abandoned cemetery on a peninsula of the lake. His former home was also only a short distance from the new departure site. In May, I attended Abilene's Western Heritage Festival and used the trip to plan our route. I used a Roads of Texas map and plotted every turn in the road from Ranger to home.

A few days before the trip, Charles called and asked if he could bring a sixteen-year-old boy with him. The boy was in his care for the summer. In his words, "He's a good kid and won't be no trouble. If he is any trouble, I will take care of it." We knew he would, so Marion and I said we could use another wrangler and cocinero's assistant.

Thursday, June 4, and Friday June 5, 1998

The Trip to Ranger

The night before our departure was unusual for early June. It was one of those hot, muggy nights that make your hair stand on end and your nerves edgy. Charles arrived at my place in Campbell just before dark with the mules in my trailer. He had to return home to get the covered wagon. He returned after dark with the mules and his young protege. The young man stood well over six feet, weighed over 200 pounds, and was wearing one of those worn out black hats that teenage *kickers* are fond of. Charles treated the mules much better than he did Gordy. Having been a friend of Charles' since boyhood, I knew that the hard-edged banter and more than a little cussin' that Gordy took concealed a fondness probably not apparent to a stranger. It was Charles' way of making a man out of him. Gordy turned out to be Jordan Brown, a football player at Highland Park High School in Dallas. Charles gives most people a nickname. When I heard about Highland Park, I wondered if he had ever been in a saddle longer than a couple of hours. However, he brought his own horse. We later learned that his grandfather owns a ranch in Colorado. Besides, Charles said he would take care of him. Seemed to me everything was going to be all right.

It was really threatening a bad storm that night, so we pulled everything under my shed, and Charles and Gordy spent the night in my barn. Couldn't coax them into the house. The rain and wind did come, bringing welcome relief from the sultry heat.

We woke to cooler weather and that rare refreshing morning in Texas after a good rain. Little did we know that this would be the last good rain till September. I was up and dressed in my hat, stampede string, tall boots, and red wild rag. Jerald arrived just after dawn. Wife Jan brought out great biscuits, bacon, orange juice, and coffee. Marion ran out of gas on the way over and was a little late. We asked if he had planned the rest of his trip as well as the drive from Cooper to Commerce. Marion (fifty-seven), Charles(fifty-two) and I (fifty-three) had left off shaving for a few days and gray beards were showing. Charles remarked that I looked like *hammered hell*. I assumed that was a compliment. We were dressed as close as possible to the period we hoped to recreate. Jerald had to be told to get rid of his sleeveless shirt before we started down the trail, and Gordy was told to forget the tee shirt. Only long sleeves on this trip.

We joked and placed bets on the weight of the mules and how long Gordy's horse's shoes would last. They looked as if the farrier had just picked up his hooves and nailed them on without worrying about fit. They were already clicking. Then we progressed to betting on how long before we would have to have a trail side funeral for the horse. He was obviously very overweight and out of shape for the trip. We loaded the two mules, Marion's horse, and Gordy's horse in my trailer behind Jerald's truck. I pulled my horse and Jerald's two horses in my other trailer behind my pickup. Marion and Charles pulled the wagon in a flat bed trailer behind Charles' pickup. Jordan was to ride with Jerald, leaving me to ride by myself. We had them all loaded before we realized that we had not planned a route for the vehicle part of the trip. Although I had done a lot of planning for the return by horseback, I hadn't worried at all about the trip by truck and trailer. We quickly looked at the maps and agreed, we thought, on a route, and took off in three trucks and three trailers.

We had traveled all of an hour before some of us got lost. I can't really say for sure who. I had made the trip a couple of times before and usually left from the north side of Dallas. That is the route I took. The other two trucks went south of Dallas. They stopped to let me see the error of my ways, but I thought I had just gotten behind and was racing ahead to catch up. By the time I realized they were not ahead of me, it was too late to turn back.

Although I had been to Ranger a few times before, it stilled seemed strange to see my somewhat unusual last name on business signs and mailboxes as I drove into town. I tried to feel the presence of my ancestors and relatives that still lived in the area that I had never met. After determining that the others had not arrived before me, I contacted cousin Calvin Ainsworth and drove to Lake Leon. I found Marion's family at a gas station, so I left them in Ranger to notify the others where to come. I unloaded the horses at the lake and waited three hours for the others to arrive. You can imagine the insults that were exchanged about getting lost. All I could say was that I arrived three hours earlier than they did—so who had the best route?

Friday, June 5, 1998

❧⚜❧

Visiting Our Great-Grandfather

Unlike Marion's and mine, Calvin's grandparents had stayed in Eastland and Callahan counties. He was a county commissioner and knew the area well. He had arranged for a park ranger to meet us with a small boat and take us to the grave site of our great-grandfather William Levin Ainsworth. Marion, his daughter Trish, Calvin, myself, and the park ranger motored out to the peninsula. Although the cemetery can be reached over land, it can't be reached by vehicle and the walk is through private property over several miles. Ashore, we climbed up the hill through heavy brush and trees. We found Old Providence Cemetery to be essentially abandoned. With cattle roaming over the peninsula, the grave markers are only partially protected by cactus, locust, mesquite and scrub oak trees. An occasional ornate and ancient cemetery fence also provided some protection from the cattle. Although unkempt and in need of repair, we found the spot to be very serene. It sits on a high spot overlooking the lake, and cool breezes manage to permeate the thick underbrush.

Marion and I had heard about our great grandfather's grave since we were boys. Even our fathers had visited the grave only when Lev was laid to rest there. Calvin had visited only a few times since the lake had made it so difficult to reach. When we started finding grave markers, I thought I had found great-grandfather William Lev's when I saw W. L. Ainsworth on a granite marker. However, the year of birth was 1877, thirty-seven years after Lev was born. Willis Ainsworth, Lev's son and our grandfather's brother, died at age 32, nine years before his father. Lev's grave is beside Willis' but is only identified by a large unmarked stone. If Calvin had not been there

William Lev Ainsworth (left) and unidentified friend

before with his father Alfred, we would never have been able to conclusively identify it. Sadly, Calvin died a few months later.

The importance of the moment and the serenity of the location were not lost on Lev's descendants. We grew silent as we were transported back in time to visit with our fathers, our grandfathers, and an imaginary meeting with the great-grandfather who died sleeping on the ground beside a

Left to right: Jim Ainsworth, Calvin Ainsworth, and Marion Ainsworth at Old Providence Cemetery.

covered wagon and whose grave is marked only by a stone. We tried to identify with a man who was born and lived approximately the same life span as
Wild Bill Hickok, Buffalo Bill Cody, and Frank and Jesse James. It seemed
incredible that he was old enough to be Butch Cassidy's father. We discussed the legend of a man killed by either Lev or his brother Hy in a gun
duel and whether either brother had gone to jail for the offense. Family lore
has it that Lev was brought to trial and cleared. I recalled that Aunt Mabel
had told me that Lev spent three years in prison for a shooting that Hy had
actually done.

I wished for more time to just sit and meditate at this isolated spot. I'm
sure that Marion felt the same need to be alone with his thoughts and to
communicate with our jointly shared past. Why was the grave marked only
by a stone with no writing? Was he estranged from his family when he died?
Why and how did he die camped beside a wagon? Did he suffer the same
fears and problems that we face today or were they worlds apart? What
advice could he give us? But it was not to be. Twilight was fast approaching
and it was necessary to return to camp before dark.

We do know that Lev was in hiding for several years but always camped
so that he could see the lamp light from his home. His children would regu-
larly take him food and supplies and return with money or other messages
from Lev. The authorities followed Papa Hiram one night when he was
making such a delivery. I remember Papa telling us that it was pitch black
that night and he was literally feeling his way to where he thought his father
would be camped. The children were instructed to just come to a certain
area and let their father find them. All of a sudden and without warning, he
felt strong arms lift him up and over a horse's withers. The horse was running at a stong gallop as he was lifted, and soon reached an all-out run. He
struggled to free himself until he heard his father whisper "It's me son."
They rode hard, but soon discovered that lawmen were in front as well as
behind them. Lev surrendered rather than put his son at risk.

I wished for more time to just sit and meditate at this isolated spot. I'm
sure that Marion felt the same need to be alone with his thoughts and to
communicate with our jointly shared past. Why was the grave marked only
by a stone with no writing? Was he estranged from his family when he died?
Why and how did he die camped beside a wagon? Did he suffer the same
fears and problems that we face today or were they worlds apart? What
advice could he give us? But it was not to be. Twilight was fast approaching
and it was necessary to return to camp before dark.

After leaving Old Providence Cemetery, we visited Staff Cemetery,
where Calvin's father, Alfred Sebastian Ainsworth is buried. We also visited
Cook Cemetery, which seemed to be dominated by Ainsworth markers. As
a county commissioner, Calvin knew every road in the county. He took us
across many cattle guards and opened many gates to get to the remote cem-
eteries. Cook Cemetery is located on a remote bluff. Although you can see
over rolling hills for miles, no sign of civilization was visible. It was moving
to be in this isolated place that I had never visited before with my last name
visible on over twenty graves. Jerald dug up a small red cactus plant on the
fringe of the cemetery and took it home. He later planted it beside my front
gate under an old bois d'arc tree.

When we arrived back at camp on the shores of Lake Leon, Charles had prepared pork chops, potatoes and all the trimmings. With Charles around, the meals just seemed to happen without effort or planning. After the meals were over, things just seemed to be put away. Before we realized it, Charles was sleeping soundly. His peaceful sleep did not last long, however. The temperature plunged to the 40's that night and the wind off the lake sent us hunting for more cover. We had not planned on anything this cool. I closed every opening in my bedroll, covered my head, and made it through the night.

Charles Horchem

Saturday, June 6, 1998

⚜

Ranger Festival and
First Day on the Trail

Woke refreshed after my first night sleeping on the ground in a bed roll—even if it was a little cold. Charles kept asking, "Has anybody ever froze to death in Ranger, Texas in June?" We were a little disorganized on this first day of travel, but Charles had potatoes, eggs and sausage going by the time we fed the stock. We managed to leave by around 9:45. We had to cover the eleven miles from Lake Leon to Ranger in time for the Old Time Country Festival. We were to be honored guests at the headquarters of the Ranger Historical Preservation Society. As soon as we were underway, our confidence began to grow. We had been joined by Marion's family including wife Pat, daughters Treva Lajaunie, Trish Chalaire and Lacy Ainsworth, and sons-in-law Randy Lajaunie, and Tommy Chalaire. Tommy rode in the wagon with Charles and got a lesson in driving mules. Charles soon renamed him Tommy Lee. Randy and the rest of the family met us occasionally in their car on this first day.

As I began to *really see* the back roads I had traveled by car, actually experiencing the ride horseback on a cool, crisp morning was about as good as it gets. I was really living the trip I had only visualized for almost two years. Jerald Thomas was riding up front with me. He had spent most of his childhood and early adulthood as a city boy in Dallas dreaming of living in the country. He had achieved that dream by moving his family to Commerce twenty years earlier, but riding his own horse alongside a covered wagon on a trip that was actually going somewhere was another dream come true for him. That old cowboy saying *If you think all men are created equal, then you have never been afoot and met a man sitting a good horse* came to mind.

We had lunch with the good people of Ranger under a tent. An Abilene television station was there to interview us about the trip, and we were entertained with several old time country songs. There was a special moment when an elderly man joined a woman on stage to sing a song about Grandpa and Grandma's new wagon. We saw evidence of the Ainsworth brand (the backward KD) registered to our great-uncle Alfred Ainsworth in 1897. When I asked Calvin about the backward KD, he said that he was told that the initials belonged to Alfred's mistress and that his wife never knew their origin.

Charles kept up his inquiries of the locals about freezing to death in Ranger in June. This is where he first learned about the *cedar hackers* and the infamous bars of Mingus. More on that later. I stepped on the bandstand and told the visitors about our planned trip. The band played *Cowboy Rides Away* as we left. Before leaving Ranger, Charles insisted that we stop at an antique and second hand store to buy extra quilts. We never needed quilts again.

Since I had traveled and planned the route, the others only briefly mentioned that home was due east as we headed due north out of Ranger. We had to go north because of famous Ranger Hill, the truck drivers' nemesis on the road heading east out of Ranger. Without a shoulder and with a significant downgrade, we would have been road kill for trucks. Besides, north was much prettier. And pretty it was as we headed into significant hills and valleys (for Texas) on our way to Strawn.

Calvin had arranged for us to stay with the Larry Herrington family our second night. Larry and his son were second and third generation ropers. Larry's dad had been a champion calf roper and he and his son were both winning team ropers. I was especially interested because team roping was to be my next endeavor. We got a look at one of Larry's father's champion calf roping saddles, won at a major event at a time when trophy saddles were a rarity. Larry was a second generation cattle rancher, but he was also raising goats because of the higher profit margin. He also said goats can survive on much less than cattle when drought comes.

As we prepared to set up camp at Larry's place I wondered about the feasibility of carrying my bedroll on my saddle. It certainly looked authentic and could have been used in the previous century, but getting off and on a horse with a bedroll, slicker, and saddlebags behind you is a little tricky. The bedroll also make it very difficult to get to your saddlebags during the day. I decided that throwing just the bedroll in the wagon tomorrow wouldn't be too great a sacrifice to authenticity. This ended our first real day on the trail. Charles cooked his usual good meal and we were all ready for our bedrolls early. True to expectations, Gordon's horse Geronimo, (also known as Red Cloud) colicked that night, and Gordy had to lose a lot of sleep walking him until he seemed out of danger.

Just as I was about to finally doze off, I heard this terrible noise a few feet from me. It sounded like a wild hog eating something that was choking him. Marion was also sitting up on his cot asking, "What the hell is that?" This was our introduction to Gordy's little snoring problem. Seems his parents had taken him to the doctor, but he would not submit to the surgery required to correct it. I guess they must have added a wing to their house with soundproof walls. We agreed that he would sleep much further away tomorrow night.

Sunday, June 7

❦

Hot Shot, Nacho, and Mingus

Jerald and I left early in his truck to look for a spot to camp on night three. While we were gone, some of the neighboring horses got mixed in with our horses and mules as Charles, Marion and Gordy were preparing the stock for departure. They averted a near disaster that saw our mules and one horse go down the highway leaving for parts unknown. Larry jumped in his truck and managed to get in front of them while Marion hastily threw on a saddle and followed on horseback. They finally managed to catch all the stock and return. What could have been a disaster had been barely avoided. They got underway late, but with everything intact.

Meanwhile, Jerald and I reached the edge of Palo Pinto Lake before finding a place to stay. We stopped at an unusual rock home at the intersection of two farm-to-market highways. It had a nice barn and corrals in back and access to water. Mrs. Johnson, the owner, was a little tentative about allowing us to camp there, but said we could ask her son. He wasn't there at the time, so we went down the road looking for another spot. We couldn't go very far, because we knew the mules and horses could only travel so far before dark. This area is sparsely populated, so we had no luck. We returned with hats in hand.

Luckily, her son was there. He introduced himself as Hot Shot Johnson. I guess Jerald and I both gave him a "you're pulling our legs" look. He smiled and explained that it was a moniker his grandfather had hung on him. He agreed to allow us to stay the night, providing he could make his mother comfortable with it. He didn't live there, but did raise cattle and tend to the place. When she came outside, she asked us if our behavior was going to be proper. We assured her it was. After she became comfortable with us and our story, she asked us if we drank. We stumbled a little, then decided to be honest and mentioned an occasional beer or a shot of Jack Daniels. We offered to completely refrain from any alcohol if it would make her more comfortable. She replied, "Oh no. I just don't like to drink alone and wanted to know if I could possibly join you." We were, of course, delighted and told her we would return well before sundown and would be happy to have her and Hot Shot join us for supper as well as a drink afterward.

Jerald and I rejoined the group just as they were leaving the Herrington's place. The ride to Strawn was again very scenic over rolling hills and valleys. Our first encounter with wildlife was an unfriendly rattlesnake. Marion and I were both carrying pistols, but he was long gone before we could get them out of our saddlebags. Probably a good thing. We could have started a real rodeo with a gunshot or two. Just down the road, we also encountered a fawn, then a bobcat. If this keeps up, we will have lots of unusual sightings to report on this trip.

Just before lunch, we met a couple of other fellows who made the trip more interesting. Don Stringer, my brother-in-law had found us and decided to ride with us for the day on Jerald's buckskin (Mr. Skip Jangles). I was riding Rowdy, my five-year-old sorrel gelding. I had owned him for three years and had ridden him five to seven times a week during those three years. He was in shape for this trip. Marion was riding his grey horse Bonner, a three-year-old gelding that he had owned just long enough to break. Jerald also brought along his three year old Palomino gelding, Pal O Nina. You already know about Gordy's Geronimo, also known as Red Cloud. The matched white mules had different names each morning. Even their owner gave them different names. I believe their real names were Clyde and Bell. But they were known variously as Casper and Jasper, Jack and Jill, Jake and Blue. Charles said he liked to call out several names so that the mules would think they had help. I digress. Back to the second fellow who made the trip more interesting.

As we topped one of the high hills, Charles' hat blew off. In a scramble to grab it, he knocked his glasses to the road. As we stopped to retrieve the broken glasses, three men in a pickup pulled up beside the wagon. One seemed to be especially thrilled to see a trail drive. It didn't seem to matter that there were no cattle. The three had spent Saturday in the Mingus bars and had obviously continued their good time well into Sunday morning. One fellow pleaded to ride on the covered wagon. He was a great fan of and expert on trivia about *Rawhide*. He named us Mr. Faver, Rowdy Yates, Wishbone, etc. Though his words were very slurred, I believe his name was Robert Munoz. He pronounced his name several times for Charles, but Charles replied, "I can't understand what you're saying, so I'm just going to call you "Nacho." That seemed to suit, so we resumed our journey with Nacho on the wagon seat with Charles. Nacho was a handsome young man, with most of his exposed skin decorated by tattoos. He confided that they were mostly jailhouse tattoos that he had acquired as a five-year guest of the state.

As luck would have it, Nacho was a cedar hacker. Charles gleefully extracted as much information as possible from Nacho about cedar hackers and the Mingus bars. Before he left with his friends, Charles promised to meet him in Mingus that night.

Besides Charles' broken glasses, Jerald had lost an antique canteen, the first of many minor casualties during the trip. We stopped in Strawn for ice and a short rest. I tied my horse to a post and went inside for ice. Rowdy had been trained well to stay tied, and I was confident enough to break my

Marion Ainsworth in downtown Strawn. Texas

rule of never tying by the reins. When I returned, I had to brag a little as he calmly stood where I had left him. Shucks, I thought, I could have probably just thrown the reins on the ground and he would have stayed ground tied—might just do that for the rest of the trip to show how well my horse behaves. My swelled head was soon to deflate, however. Just as I was reaching to untie him, Charles made a slight move to his left. That horse pulled back and broke both reins.

Mingus was only about five miles from Strawn, but it was the wrong direction. I had been through Mingus on my scouting trip, and called it the town with seventeen bars and only one open. Charles insisted on calling Mingus Meridian and mildly complained when we didn't have time to go only five miles out of our way. That ten-mile round trip would take three hours and would make us late for our campsite. He kept saying that he wanted a chance to put on his "pointy-toed boots" and have a good time.

We arrived right on time at the Johnson place. Hot Shot and his mother were there to greet us. It was threatening rain as we arrived, and we took

Hot Shot Johnson and his mother.

shelter in the barn just as the thundershower arrived. Having thrown our saddles and bedrolls into the dry barn, we thought the hay looked very inviting as a place to sleep. We asked Hot Shot if it would be all right if we slept in the barn. He said, "Sure, but be real careful if you pull down any bales of hay. I killed four rattlers in here so far this year." Marion and I just glanced at each other. It was not necessary to say that we would find some other way to stay dry.

True to her word, Mrs. Johnson joined us and brought us a potato salad. We all enjoyed another great meal. Hot Shot explained to us that his mother's maiden name was Ringo and she was a descendant of Johnny Ringo. Soon after supper, it was time for Don, Tommy and Jerald to head home. All wanted to stay for at least a couple more days, but duties back home called. They took my pickup, Jerald's truck and trailer, and Don's pickup—leaving us only Charles' pickup and my trailer. I had been reluctant to keep a truck and trailer because of the inconvenience of moving it from camp to camp, but we decided it might be handy in case of emergency. Later, it did come in handy.

After the meal, Charles said, "Since it's raining and we can't do anything else, let's go down to Meridian (translate Mingus) and see if we can see what those cedar hackers look like." We all declined—several times. I finally relented, but only on the condition that we would return on my say-so and that would be quick if it looked dangerous. Hot Shot overheard us talking about Mingus and related a story about prior visits he used to make there as a younger man. One ended with his head being cut open. When he finally got home, he was in such bad shape that his wife had to remove his boots. They were filled with blood. "I wouldn't go there if I were you," he advised. But, this was a once-in-a-lifetime trip and we were not going to have any regrets of things we did not do.

Charles cleaned up a little and put on his "pointy-toed boots," which were not really pointed, but I wasn't taking the trip seriously enough to bother. I left just as I was. I planned on entering the bar, seeing the menacing eyes of cedar hackers and turning around and leaving. The story related to us by Nacho and others in Ranger was that cedar hackers bring their axes to the bar and prop them up against the outside wall. When trouble erupts, which it always does, they go outside to get them. I wanted no contact with anybody in a bar who was an expert at wielding an axe.

We arrived in Mingus and found the *City Limits*, the only bar that was open. I had only been joking about the seventeen bars with one open, but it had turned out to be correct. It was a Sunday night, and you couldn't really tell if the other bars were out of business or just closed. I had heard on my scouting trip that Mingus has been a week-end gathering point for Ranger,

Baird and several surrounding towns when it was the only place where liquor could be obtained for miles around. People came for miles around to dance and imbibe. When surrounding towns voted wet, Mingus declined and the bars were pretty much taken over by cedar hackers. Thus the seventeen bars in a town with population of less than a thousand.

When we left the truck, Charles warned me "If trouble starts, you leave first, crank the truck and I will be right behind you." Having known Charles for almost forty years, I knew that this was not idle chatter. Charles is a big, but nimble fellow. Being basically good natured didn't stop him from enjoying an occasional good fight in our younger years. Weighing about one hundred pounds less, I had no such inclination. Any appetite I may have had for fisticuffs had long ago been satisfied. I hoped he was too old to enjoy one now.

Charles was disappointed to see no axes outside the door. I was afraid they might already be inside. As we entered, we looked through the smoky haze for cedar hackers with axes. We attracted a little attention, but not nearly as much as we would have somewhere else. Charles was wearing his big hat and was colorfully dressed with his jeans tucked in black alligator boots and colorful suspenders. I was still wearing chinks, spurs, a large red wild rag, and a buck knife protruded from my exposed boot tops. Another smaller knife hung from a scabbard on my belt. These knives were strictly for utilitarian trail ride purposes, but I suddenly wished I had left them at camp. I also became very conscious of how I must look and more important, how I must smell after three days on a horse. A few cedar hackers, including our friend Nacho, were in the bar. Also included were Nacho's father, who sat immobile at the bar during our entire visit, a few assorted other patrons, and the requisite number of drunks. None seemed hostile.

Charles struck up an acquaintance with most of the patrons. We were amazed that Nacho was still able to stand. He had, however, lost most of his ability to speak. When Charles took his beer of choice and set a different brand in front of him, it confused him for the rest of the night. We had a couple of beers, passed the time with Nacho and other folks, and went back to the campsite. When we left the bar, I was relieved, but somehow disappointed. Turns out that cedar hackers are just guys who hack cedar trees into posts. They rarely hack people.

Back at camp, it was raining again. I went into the barn for my bedroll, thought about the dry hay, then the rattlesnakes, and threw my bedroll in the bottom of my trailer. It had transported three horses on the way out and had not been cleaned out yet. My bedroll still bears the stains. In case you ever wonder, trailers with tops but open sides don't deter much rain.

Monday, June 8

The Brazos and
Oaks Crossing Slim

I felt better than I expected to after sleeping in a wet trailer filled with horse manure all night. Hot Shot came out on his way to work to see us off. We made good time in leaving camp that morning. We were down to the core group of myself, Marion, Charles and Gordy. I knew that it would be tough to make it to the Brazos before dark, but I sure wanted to spend the night on the river. We crossed the bridge at Lake Palo Pinto and entered Palo Pinto, county seat of Palo Pinto County. As we passed the courthouse, a lady emerged and asked up to please circle the courthouse, so all the folks inside could get a look. We obliged.

We were starting to notice the heat today for the first time. The temperature had climbed into the 90's. We took Pleasant Valley Road just outside Palo Pinto to the Brazos. Having driven it before, I knew we were in for a long haul on a red rock and occasional dirt road that seems to go nowhere. There were almost no signs. I also knew that we would have to ford the Brazos since there was no bridge on this road. By four o'clock, the others were beginning to wonder if we were really going anywhere. The sun was bearing down, and we couldn't take the time to rest if we were going to camp on the river's edge. By six, we were on a definite downward path to the river bottom. Our spirits picked up and an occasional *Braaaaazoos* yell could be heard. Soon, we could smell the water.

Rio de los Brazos de Dios (River of the Arms of God) was the original name for the Brazos. Hiram and Eva must have felt the name was appropriate when they reached this point. My mind went back to that original wagon trip. Although we knew that the remainder of the trip would not take the same path as our ancestors, they surely crossed the Brazos and this was the likely spot. I began to transport myself back in time to their arrival and tried to become my grandfather. I could see the children wading in the cool, welcome water and Hiram and Eva feeling proud to have reached this landmark. Marion expressed similar thoughts. Charles, probably born a hundred years too late like Marion and myself, definitely felt the spirit. Gordy was just glad to be near water.

Finally, we could hear the running water. I was relieved to see that the river was low enough for us to cross. When I had been here by car, it was definitely too high. I was told that water was occasionally released without warning from Possum Kingdom Lake, and the river rose too high to cross. That would mean literally turning around and retracing our half-day journey. Worse, it would have meant crossing the Brazos on a highway bridge instead of fording it. Luck was with us.

As we approached the water's edge, we knew this was a pivotal moment for the trip. We saw some folks watching the water on the other side. I took my camera and Marion's over to them and asked them to take some pictures as we crossed. As we entered the softly running current, we felt cool

Crossing the Brazos

Marion, Jim, Charles, and Jordan on the banks of the Brazos River.

and refreshed. We reflected on hundreds of movies we had seen where wagons and cattle had crossed rivers under similar conditions. I watched helplessly as a dutch oven hanging under the wagon was swept downstream (later recovered). When we reached the other side, even non sentimental Charles said "Ainsworth, if those pictures don't turn out, we're all coming back here to repeat that crossing." He then took off his boots and waded waist deep into the water, clothes and all.

I wanted to join him for my first bath in four days, but Hot Shot and his wife Margie drove up just as I started off with my boots. They brought a wonderful looking Hawaiian Pineapple Cake. Margie also brought samples of her beautiful art work done with turkey feathers. She is a very talented artist and paints all sorts of wildlife scenes on turkey feathers—then frames them. I asked if she could do a scene of us crossing the Brazos. She said she would try. That turkey feather painting now hangs at *Across the Creek* (my barn) and is one of my most treasured possessions. Marion, Charles and Gordy each have one.

Although we were dog tired, I traveled back to the Johnson Ranch to pick up Charles' pickup and my trailer. I had not wanted to bring them along, and at this point, I thought I was right. I didn't want to get in a car; I wanted to get in that river. The trip back seemed longer than the trip by wagon (and was considerably longer in miles). When I finally returned, the cake had turned to mush in the heat and humidity. I had looked forward to having a piece of that cake. Everyone was clean from a bath in the river, and it was dark. I was getting used to eating trail dust and being dirty, but nothing was going to keep me from bathing in the Brazos. I stripped down, got a bar of soap, and waded out into the river.

Just as I was really feeling good, a pickup came along on our side of the river. It was traveling about sixty in an area where most vehicles would fall apart from the bumps and holes at half that speed. It hit the river at full speed and splashed water on both sides. For a split second, I thought it had completely submerged. Incredibly, the engine didn't even stall and it trudged on across. It was immediately followed by a small car bouncing along at high speed. It careened to a skidding stop just beside the water. A woman got out, shook her fist at the car and began to sob. Well now, this was interesting! Charles was liking this campsite more and more. He went over to offer any help he could. That distracted her long enough for me to sneak over to an area shielded from the moonlight and put on some clothes. It seems that the woman was chasing her husband and another woman. Charles and Gordy found this very entertaining, but Marion and I were just too tired to see anything but an interruption to an otherwise pastoral scene.

Very tired, I placed my bedroll far downstream so that I could possibly hear if the horses wandered that way. I just lay back and and enjoyed the sound of the running river. I could hear Marion and Charles talking deep into the night, but I only heard patches of their conversation.

I thought of *Goodbye to a River,* a book by John Graves that I had been somehow driven to buy and read three or four years before I ever thought of making this trip. It is a narrative about the author's journey by small canoe down the Brazos in 1957 just before it was dammed and civilization began to spoil it. Since this was not my usual type of reading material, I wondered why I was compelled to buy a book published in 1959. I had never contemplated anything about crossing the Brazos at the time I purchased it. Now I knew why. John Graves talked about the Brazos and a history of people along its banks including Comanches, Kiowas, settlers, warriors and wanderers. As I drifted off to sleep, thoughts of those people and my ancestors took away tired irritability and replaced it with calm serenity. I couldn't remember if John Graves had mentioned Oaks Crossing. When I returned home, I found these words in his book.

Near the Oakes Crossing where the old road between Weatherford and Palo Pinto used to hit the river, the water's surface was much as I remembered the surface of the classic Test, in the south-English chalk country, from once when I stood there on a bridge watching the big, incredibly uniform trout at their feeding stations over the gravel. Smooth, with little swirls forming everywhere and drifting downstream to disappear, a dry-fly man's reverie. . . . The Brazos runs wide there, with a large gravel bottom about a foot and a half down like the Tests, and that was why they were alike.

As I awoke on the sands of the river's edge, I noticed that the mornings were getting progressively warmer and the days hotter. I also noticed the unsightly trappings of man's cruelty to his own environment in the beer bottles and trash in the brush. I had difficulty in the dark of the night before finding a good place to hobble or tie Jerald's two horses and my own because of broken bottles in the trees and brush. Charles had a good breakfast going as we fed the stock. We were enjoying eggs and bacon and listening to the soothing sound of a running river when we saw a man approaching us in a deliberate stride. We were looking into the rising sun and had to shield our eyes to get a good look. We wondered momentarily if he might be going to ask us to leave. He didn't seem surprised to see a covered wagon sporting Texas and United States flags, two white mules, five saddle horses, three older men and a boy camped on the river. "You fellows seen anything of a young stud around here?" Charles said he had seen a couple of horses peeking through the brush on the river's west side about two-hundred yards downstream just about daylight. "Can't be mine. No way for them to get over there."

The man appeared to be in his late seventies or early eighties, although his age would be hard to judge. His skin had seen a lot of sun, though it was barely wrinkled. He had that look of being aged, not old. His eyes were alert, intense and bespoke intelligence. There was no excess fat on his body, and I would wager that there never had been. I always seem to notice a man's boots, since I used to sell them for a living. His were soft tan calfskin. They weren't polished, but only showed a light coat of dust. They weren't exactly scuffed, just worn in the right places. They seemed to form a comfortable mold around his feet. They were, well, just right. He wore Wranglers that hung well on his body, not too loose nor too tight. His shirt was a simple western one with two pockets and snaps. Not too fancy, not too plain. He wore a 3 1/4" brim silver belly Stetson or Resistol. I couldn't tell which for sure. Again, it was worn well and well worn, creased good, but not used up.

He began to study the wagon and identified it correctly as a Studebaker. Then he turned his attention to the mules and horses, complimented those that deserved it and kept silent about the ones that didn't. He then inquired about our destination and purpose. When we mentioned that we were from Northeast Texas, he inquired if we knew Jay Palmer, horse and cattle trader. Both Marion and I knew him by reputation and sight, but not well. Since then I have become well acquainted with Jay. He supplies cattle for team ropings that I attend.

We repeatedly asked him to join us for breakfast, but he wouldn't even take a cup of coffee. He had struck a pose very familiar to Marion and myself and probably most people who grew up in any rural area of Texas. He leaned down, bent his left knee out in front, put most of his weight on his right heel, and rested his arms alternately on the tops of his legs while he used his pocket knife to alternately whittle and illustrate his conversation in the sand. He told us stories about cattle drives to Ft. Worth, selling mules, horses and cattle at the Ft. Worth Stockyards. He also ran race horses at Ruidosa and Raton, New Mexico and said he had started spending a lot of his summers there to beat the heat. He told of growing up around the Brazos and "Payla Pinta." I knew I had heard Palo Pinto pronounced this way before, but couldn't remember where. Back to John Graves' book, chapter seven. Here he relates a story about an old timer living on the Brazos and pronouncing it "Payla Pinta." A few months after our trip, Marion called me to tell me that John Wayne pronounced it the same way in the great movie, *Red River*.

Based on his stories, our visitor had to be at least seventy-five. However, he kept that same kneeling position for over forty-five minutes. When it was time to go, he arose without a groan or hesitation. I asked him if he was familiar with *Goodbye to a River*, since he had told us he grew up and had lived most of his life on the Brazos. He said he certainly had read the book. He said the story about the family with pigs was based on his brother's family. Another reason for buying that book. I asked his name and he handed me a business card. It said, J. M. Gill (Oaks Crossing Slim)— Quality Horses—Buy-Sell. As he gracefully and purposefully walked away, Marion looked at me with a twinkle in his eye and grinned. I knew what he was going to say before he said it. "Jim, who just visited us?" "Papa Hiram," I replied as I walked off to saddle the horses for another day on the trail.

Tuesday, June 9, 1998

❦

Horse Trouble, Millsap, and the Double W

Saddling up and heading out from the Brazos wasn't as easy as the day before. When I went to get Jerald's two horses, both were gone. I didn't get too excited because I had hobbled the palomino and tied the buckskin to a sapling in the dark of the night before. I had fed them only a little more than an hour before. I was out of shouting distance, so I didn't bother telling the others. I just started tracking. About a hundred yards down the trail, I found the hobbles. Pal had small ankles and hooves and had worked his way out of them. A little further, I found the buckskin's halter and lead rope. So now I had two horses loose in rough brush country beside a river two hundred miles from home. They might have "free rein" all the way to Granbury. I thought of Oaks Crossing Slim, a native of the area who had lost a horse of his own. If he couldn't find his, what chance did I have of finding two? I also thought of Papa Hiram and his going back home to collect old Prince. The trail was fresh, and I just didn't believe that these horses would have gone far. Far is relative when you are on foot, however. Just as I was about to return to saddle Rowdy for a long hunt, I saw both horses stopped at some impenetrable brush. I walked right up, haltered one and tied the other with a makeshift string and brought them back. Walking three miles in the morning heat had not started my day right.

Back at camp, I expected everyone to be saddled and waiting for me. However, Marion had found a lump on his horse's withers that looked menacing. He couldn't be saddled. Injury to man and injury to animals had been

our primary concerns when planning this trip. This was our first real problem. The lump looked like what Arch and Teadon had called fistalo or
fiscalo. That was colloquial for fistula or fistulous withers or poll evil. In a
word, it was bad. This condition could be dangerous for both men and animals and could lead to six months of isolated treatment if the condition was
caused by bacteria. I told Marion that I wouldn't blame him if he wanted to
take the horse and head home. That was why we had the pickup and trailer.
He was understandably disappointed that the horse was unlikely to finish
the trip and would possibly die. He looked at me and just nodded. I knew
that thoughts of turning back for any reason other than death or serious
injury had been left at home. At our ages, both Marion and I knew we
couldn't afford to take any thought of quitting along. We would finish this
trip come hell or high water.

Marion loaded Bonner and left to look for a veterinarian in
Weatherford. He was to meet us later on the trail. The rest of us reluctantly
left the Brazos and headed out of the river bottom toward Millsap. We were
all worried about Bonner, but knew that our forebears had withstood much
greater tragedy and kept going. I turned my thoughts to the history of the
country we were in and how we would soon head north away from the original trail taken by Hiram and Eva and their children. Daddy and Arch had
often told stories about watering the horses in downtown Dallas. We had
briefly considered heading through downtown, but knew that getting there
through the traffic arteries would be dangerous and not much fun. Today,
though, it was likely that we were very close to their original route.

I also knew that we were close to the *Goodnight-Loving Trail* begin-
ning point around old Fort Belknap. Maybe we could return later and follow
that trail with some cattle. Tomorrow, we would be near the grave of Bose
Ikard in Weatherford. Bose was the most trusted companion of Charles
Goodnight and assumed to be the inspiration for for Danny Glover's Joshua
Deets character in Larry McMurtry's *Lonesome Dove*. Bose's stone in
Weatherford cemetery says:

> Served with me four years on Goodnight-Loving Trail, never
> shirked a duty or disobeyed an order, rode with me in many
> stampedes, participated in three engagements with Comanches.
> Splendid behavior—C. Goodnight.

Marion rejoined us before noon just outside Millsap. He had the horse's
swollen lump tested but wouldn't know the results for a couple of days.
Thanks to Jerald, we had a couple of extras to ride, anyway. Since he was
already in the truck, Marion went ahead to find lodging for our fifth night
on the trail. We were entering a slightly more populated area in cutting

horse country now, and there were more county roads to confuse. Marion took a wrong turn, but the result was fortuitous for us. He came back with Ted Williams, a genial teacher who had offered us a place to camp for the night at his Double W ranch between Weatherford and Millsap. We could tell Ted appreciated the value of what we were trying to accomplish by following in the steps of our ancestors. Since this was Marion's first night as *designated beggar,* he was very pleased to find such a congenial host.

Ted's Double W ranch was just off Old Millsap highway, a road I had not scouted. He told us that it was the oldest highway still in use in Texas and was built in 1918. That coincidence convinced Marion and me that our ancestors were very likely some of the first to travel on it. The ranch is distinctive in many ways, but a barn with the Texas flag painted on top emphasizes the obvious interest and pride that our hosts took in the history of our state. We were introduced to Ted's wife Debbie, son Thad and mother Dorothy. Ted then led us to the top of a hill where corrals and water tanks for our stock were waiting. Best of all, there was a big tree for shade and lots of nice grass to sleep on. We took our first showers that night courtesy of a camp shower thingumajig that I had brought along but never thought we would use. We hung it from a tree limb and stood under it That clean water felt good. As we settled down for the night, we noticed that old Geronimo was colicky again. Gordy walked the horse as we gave instructions to him from our seats. We finally settled into our bedrolls to enjoy the soft grass and the cool breeze on top of that hill.

Double W Ranch, Millsap, Texas

Wedesday, June 10

❧

The Parker County Courthouse and a Springtown Dairy

I continued to be pleasantly surprised at how easy it was to arise at the crack of dawn. When you are looking straight up at the sky, you just come alive at dawn. Charles surprised us with fried doughnuts to complement our usual breakfast fare. Dorothy lives just across the road from Ted and his family. Before we left the Williams, she showed us the impressive family collection of antiques, family heirlooms and representations of old Texas and family history that she protects in a separate building behind her house. Sharing these items was a special time for us all, but the trail to Weatherford beckoned. We took pictures of everyone in front of the "Texas" barn before heading out on the historic highway. I remembered this country well from my scouting trip, and I knew we were in for some beautiful Texas scenery. We passed splendid ranches, most of which were used for raising and training cutting horses. As we were getting further east, the oaks were getting a little bigger. "Where the West begins" came to mind, only in reverse.

As we neared downtown Weatherford, the Parker County courthouse came into view. Traffic goes in a circle around the downtown square and it was pretty busy around noontime. Charles motioned for me to come close to the wagon and told me that he was going to drive the mules over the curb, through the shrubs and trees, inside the street lamps and onto the neatly manicured courthouse lawn. "Get your camera ready," he announced. Had it been anyone else, I would have thought they were joking—but not

Parker County Courthouse

Charles. I never questioned his sincerity. I did briefly wonder who would feed the stock while we were in the courthouse jail. Although the sun was shining, we were getting a few drops of rain. We entered the continuous circle of cars going around the courthouse just as if we were one of them. For some reason, all of our stock seemed to be nervous that morning. The mules were throwing their heads, and the saddle horses were prancing as if they knew they were the center of attention. I rode Rowdy onto an elevated concrete median, took the camera from my saddlebags and focused just as the wagon drove onto the lawn. Although my horse was trying to turn in circles and get back with the group, I managed to get a couple of good shots of the courthouse with the wagon and other outriders. We then calmly left downtown to avoid arrest.

Time did not permit us to visit Bose Ikard's grave. Don Edwards, my favorite cowboy singer, also lives near Weatherford. I had hoped to get a glimpse of his SevenShoux Ranch. Red Steagall, another great singer and official cowboy poet of Texas, also has his ranch on the outskirts of Weatherford. Maybe on our next trip.

Ted graciously agreed to follow Marion to our next approximate camp-site and return him so that he could ride the entire way with the group. I was *designated beggar* for the day again, so when we reached the truck and trailer I went ahead to find a campsite. The road to Springtown from Weatherford goes almost due north and has some great high spots with beautiful views of the valleys below. As usual, we avoided interstate or state highways and stayed on Old Springtown Road. This was the first day that I encountered problems finding a place to stay. As we got further east, people and houses became more abundant, but fewer had barns and corrals and places to water the stock. I drove deep into a canyon to a ranch house that was very secluded and almost hidden from view. I talked to a lady who owned the ranch with her husband, but she was a little uncomfortable with offering us a place to camp overnight. Driving further down the road, I stopped at another likely spot and spoke to an elderly couple. They sent me back to their son's dairy that I had just passed. There I met Rodney Hinkle. He was a little wary, but too nice to turn us away. He said we could spend the night on his brother Bob Hinkle's place just across from his dairy. It had no corrals or a natural campsite, and water was quite a way off. Also, we had to go rather far off the road to reach it. However, this was about our only option and I took it.

As I returned to join the group, I saw the husband of the secluded ranch lady coming out of his driveway and stopped to see if I could improve on our possibilities. His ranch seemed to have a great campsite. He said we could camp there, but I sensed that we would be an intrusion. We were deep in the canyon discussing it when he looked over the canyon wall at a fast approaching storm. "That settles it. We are going to get a heavy rain, and you would never be able to get out of here."

By the time I got back to my truck, it was pouring buckets and raining horizontally and vertically. I drove back to meet the others. I found the wagon parked on a hilltop. Gordy was standing outside in the rain holding the horses and wearing my slicker. I guessed that he was getting some more education. Marion and Charles were in the wagon as wind gusts strained the bows and pushed the canvas together. I was concerned that the whole sheet would fly away. They later claimed that they had to move from side to side to keep the wagon from being blown over. I felt guilty sitting in the pickup dry while they weathered the elements, but that guilt soon proved to be a waste of time. As the rain let up, I ventured to the wagon to chastise Gordy for stealing my slicker and to see how much damage the contents of the wagon had suffered. I found Marion and Charles inside in very high spirits. Seems they had been continuing our nightly tradition of "Let me buy you a drink. No, I'll buy you a drink," alternating with "I'll hold the gun on you while you take a drink, then you hold the gun on me while I take a drink". They were dry and happy and only slightly interested in where we had to spend the night.

Since my saddle was soaked and we were fairly close anyway, I just drove back to see what I could do with a muddy campsite. I met Julie Hinkle as I was opening the first gate to go through the mud to our campsite. She and Rodney took pity on us and said we could sleep in the hay barn providing we would not get in the way of the tractor they used to pick up the large bales and feed before dawn. I thanked them and pulled my trailer to the side of the barn. I strung rope inside the barn to hang our wet clothes and saddles from and did as much preparation as I could.

I still had some time before the others arrived, so I visited the dairy barn as they milked the cows. We had a dairy when I was a boy, so it brought back memories. As the wagon and horses approached, you could

The Hinkle Dairy, Springtown, Texas

sense growing excitement in the Hinkle family. Their sons were excited and the parents were pleased to be part of our adventure. Brother Bob was called over for a visit.

When the wagon arrived , Charles methodically went ahead with supper preparations, undeterred by the wet conditions. I had noticed Charles' planning before, but on this night I really admired him. He had frozen some soup before the trip and kept it preserved during the hot days behind us. We had soup and cornbread that were some of the best I have ever eaten. I don't know how much effect the wet and cooler conditions had on the taste, but it was a memorable meal. We invited the Hinkles to join us, but they were busy with the day's chores. When Bob arrived, he insisted on providing us with meat and vegetables from his own stock to enjoy on the rest of the trip. He was amazed at how far we had come.

As we prepared for bed, Tommy Chalaire joined us again. He had been very reluctant to leave in the first place and had arranged his personal schedule to join us again. We had a choice of mud outside or hay inside that night and we chose hay. Nobody said anything about rattlers and I enjoyed my first night on a soft bed of hay since the ride began.

Thursday, June 11

❦

The Spains and Wise County

Marion had called a couple of times to check on the results of the tests on Bonner. The vets had determined that it wasn't fistula, at least not the bacterial kind. No matter what the results, it was clear that he would require a few days' rest. He decided to return him to my pasture for recuperation at the first opportunity. Meanwhile, we would tie him to the wagon. Hopefully, he would recover enough to finish with us.

We were awakened early by the familiar sound of dairy cows moving and preparing to enter the dairy barn. We had breakfast and began saddling and harnessing. We enjoyed watching from the barn as the Hinkles moved fifty or so Holsteins into a pasture as the rising sun started to reflect off the mud pools from yesterday's rain. We said our goodbyes and headed toward Springtown, Wise County, and Decatur. We stopped on the town square of Springtown and did a little window shopping in the unusual shops we found there. Had a short conversation with Moe Headrick in his Old West Saddle Shop. He had a unique interest in our trip. He was a stunt man and double in lots of films, mostly westerns. I knew his name sounded familiar, but I couldn't place him. When I returned home, I found a business card he had given me many years before. I still don't know where our paths crossed before.

We entered Wise County just after leaving Springtown. A reporter from the Springtown paper followed us out of town and we talked with her briefly. We don't know if we made the paper, however. We didn't usually have regular stops for dinner, but just stopped and snacked at places that offered shade, quiet and a good view. As we made our first stop that day,

Jim and Rowdy breaking camp at the Spain Ranch

Charles Horchem and Mary Lois Spain leaving the Spain Ranch.

Marion discovered a hole in his saddle bags. A treasured nickel plated .22 caliber pistol had been lost. We retraced our steps but were not lucky enough to find it.

I somehow inherited the *designated beggar* job again today. I drove the mules most of the day with Tommy and Gordy as outriders. Marion and Charles had returned to get the pickup and trailer when it started getting close to time to find a campsite. We hailed a passing pickup with two young ladies and a child inside. We asked the driver if she knew of anyone who could accommodate us. She said she didn't. However, her young passenger volunteered her family's place just up the road. She was enthusiastic and welcoming, but I guessed her to be about sixteen. I wanted to talk to her parents first. She assured me it would be all right, but I insisted on seeing them first. She gave me directions, and I put Rowdy into a short lope to reach their ranch. The parents were not at home, but an aunt was. She assured me that we would be welcome. As I rejoined the others, Vicki Spain was passing the time of day with Tommy and Gordy. She was the mother and graciously confirmed her daughter's hospitality. She gave us directions to a circle of trees and a nearby pool where we could water our stock. Fol-

Jim and Jordan watering stock at the Spain Ranch.

lowing her directions, we went around a couple of cattle guards and soon found the spot. It was a good campsite with lots of green grass and a nice clump of trees for tying our horses. I usually hobbled Rowdy at night, but we tied the others. With stock tended, to we unrolled our bedding and set up camp.

Word of our trip had reached Rick Vanderpool, then publisher of the *Commerce Journal*, and he had obtained a copy of the maps we had left for family members and friends who wished to join us. As we prepared our camp, Rick arrived with some cigars and a bottle of good sippin' whiskey.

Charles and Marion periodically sneaked around and broke the trail boss rules about the use of phones on the trip. One phone call led to Charles having to sign some papers before our return. They were brought to us by his son Dutch Horchem, and Gordy's father, Tyler Brown. Seems that Charles and Tyler had swapped sons for the summer. Charles had also ordered some liquid refreshments to be brought by them from Dallas. Charles pleased everyone with a great meal of chicken fried steak and fried potatoes. We then sat around smoking our cigars, sipping, and reliving the events of the trail ride thus far.

Friday, June 12

◆━━━◆◆◆◆◆━━━◆

Decatur, Stoney, Party Barn and the Indian Vision

The grass around our campsite was extremely wet from dew the next morning. It was a crystal clear morning and the sun reflected off the dewy grass. We were joined for coffee by Ed and Vicki Spain and their lovely daughter Mary Lois, who had offered the initial invitation. They were joined by friend Sue Grantham. Seems Ms. Grantham was an amateur photographer and had already visited our campsite before daylight to take some shots. Since we had not seen her, we immediately started wondering what those shots might reveal. She caught up with us a day later and kindly brought us copies of some of the best photos taken during the entire trip. Mary Lois rode on the wagon seat with Charles as far as the main road as we pulled away toward Decatur.

Rick Vanderpool had done some scouting around the Decatur square the day before while searching for us. He had made contact with Don and Wanda Perkins, proprietors of a unique store on the Decatur square. Wanda was very interested in all things historic, so she asked that we come by her store as we passed through town. Decatur is also home to the famous Wise County Courthouse. We made a circle around the courthouse and stopped in front of the store. Wanda awaited us in period costume, something that would have been worn in the era of covered wagons. The local chamber of commerce representative and a reporter from the local newspaper were also there to greet us. We visited with them and posed for many photos.

Left unattended, Rowdy decided to climb the high sidewalk and enter the welcome air conditioning of the Perkins store. I stopped him before he went inside. As I stepped inside the store myself, I noticed that paintings by Buck Taylor (best known as Newly O'Brien on *Gunsmoke* and as Turkey Creek Johnson in *Tombstone*) were much in evidence. I knew that Buck lived nearby, and the employees thought I was Buck when I walked in. I absorbed the compliment and headed back to mount standing just a little taller and straighter than before. As we started to ride away, I noticed Marion lying in the middle of the street underneath his horse. Seems he missed his stirrup when he started to mount, causing both feet to slide on the pavement and putting him flat of his back underneath Jerald's buckskin. Fortunately, nothing but his pride was hurt. Unfortunately, nobody got a photo.

As we left the Decatur square just before noon, the temperature had climbed well into the 90's. I knew that we were in for probably the worst day's ride of the trip. My scouting had determined that Highway 380 was our only choice. This section of roadway seems to be the main route for trucks escaping from hell and leaving at high rates of speed. Having thus far restricted ourselves to county or farm to market roads in sparsely popu-

Rowdy in downtown Decatur, Texas

Gordy, Jim, Marion and Wanda Perkins in Decatur, Texas

lated areas, the bombardment of sights, sounds and smells of civilization at its worst made us a little edgy for the next five hours or so. On several blind hills with only a small shoulder on the road, we also knew that we were in some danger. We put riders far back from the wagon and far in front to signal vehicles that we were slow-moving interlopers. They paid no attention other than to honk their horns in an attempt to scare the mules. It didn't work, though. Clyde and Bell had already traveled over 170 miles, and a few trucks weren't going to jangle their nerves.

When we stopped once to untangle a lead rope from the wagon axle, a truck stopped a hundred yards in front of us. The driver started walking back. I was on my back under the wagon when I looked up to see the face of one of my closest neighbors and a good friend, Ralph Stroope. How ironic that two people who live less than a mile apart should run into each other this far from home. It was too hot to visit long and we could barely hear a shouted conversation because of the noise from the traffic.

Tommy seemed to be standing in his stirrups a lot of late and seemed to seriously want to drive the wagon. We took pity on his sore posterior and let him drive the mules while Charles went ahead for supplies and to be on the lookout for a campsite. It was clear to me that we wanted to camp as far from 380 as possible, so I started traveling the country roads to the south of

380. I stopped at a couple of likely places, but found nobody home. On my third try, a knock on the door brought a pretty young lady of preschool age to the door. She went to get the lady of the house who said she did not have the facilities to accommodate us, but sent me to her neighbors. As I thanked her and left the porch, I heard the young girl exclaim "That man was wearing a gun!" She had mistaken the knife on my belt for a holstered gun. That was a reminder of how I must look to strangers.

As I approached the hilltop farm that I had been directed to, I saw a fellow plowing a pasture in the distance. I knocked on the door and got no answer. As I was about to leave, a lady drove up and rolled down her car window. I blurted out my mission. "A covered wagon, four horses and four men are a few hours behind me. We've come from Ranger and are headed toward a small community called Shiloh. We're looking for a place to stay overnight." Janie Hull surveyed me with a slow look that took in everything from my boots to my hat. Her eyes showed amusement as well as confidence. "You might have found it," she declared without hesitation. "You fellows drink and raise hell?"

Having heard this question before, I assured her we would not. "Well, you may not like it here then, cause we generally do." I laughed and quickly amended myself and said we could readily adapt to any situation our hosts provided. I could see that her mind was working rapidly on how this interruption to her day could be made into fun. "Get in the car" she ordered. "Excuse me?" I thought I had heard her wrong. "Get in. I want to show you to someone." Thinking she was going to drag me off to a neighbor to show what the cat had drug in from the side of the road, I was a little taken aback, but not much. Her cheerfulness and mischievous demeanor told me that I was in for some fun. Without a word to her husband Royce, who happened to be the fellow plowing, she left in her Explorer with a man who had been horseback for a week and showed it. I was obviously a complete stranger, also. We drove by several homes and places looking for the person she wanted me to meet. We went to downtown Stoney. I knew that we were in the area of Ponder, but had never heard of Stoney. It is a small town noteworthy for its unique buildings and preservation of the past. Finally, we pulled up in front of one of the most interesting log cabins I had ever seen. I studied it from the outside, while Janie knocked on the door of the home next to the log cabin. Nobody home. We were at the home of Mr. and Mrs. Bill Marquis and the log cabin was the oldest such structure inhabited by other than Native Americans in Texas. She promised to return us there later for a tour.

Back at the Hull place, Janie showed me the inside of the barn behind one of the two houses. It was a huge barn with complete living quarters on the second floor. A large hall ran through the center. The hall was immaculately clean and decorated like a combination old time dance hall, restaurant and grange meeting place. Beautifully rustic and western tables were covered with checkered tablecloths. Huge doors opened at both ends to let in prevailing breezes from the hilltop. Just being in the place lifted my spirits. The east side of the hall contained places for machinery and equipment, livestock and the things barns are usually associated with. The west side, however, contained a complete chef's dream. It was a complete commercial kitchen with walk-in coolers, a huge ice machine, commercial stoves and ovens. The walk-in cooler had beer on tap complete with longhorn steer horns for tap handles. There seemed to be enough plates, bowls, saucers, utensils, etc. . . . to feed a small army. Janie's son Morgan is a well-known chef. At that time, he was working with On the Border restaurants as an experimental chef. Music to my ears. "Morgan will probably want to cook for you all." I assured her that we had our own cook and invited them to join us. "Well, if Morgan doesn't want to cook, we will join you. If he does, you all will eat with us." By this time, I knew better than to argue. Her generosity was sincere.

As I rode back to inform the others, I was elated to have been so lucky to find such friendly people and such a terrific place to spend the night. This deep into our trail ride experience, I knew that more than luck was bringing us into contact with so many wonderful people and offering us such memorable experiences. When I finally reached the wagon, I found that Charles had also found us a place to stay the night—and it was about two hours closer. The group was exhausted from our most grueling day and seemed to lean toward the earlier stop. Charles had found a fellow baling hay beside 380. He had a nice barn, a corral and a stock tank. Usually, we would have considered this an ideal find. Today, however, it was definitely in distant second place. I told them we had to continue to travel for at least an hour or so more to reach the Hull Place. I couldn't convey the sense of welcome that I had felt, but their ears perked up when I mentioned the big ice machine and the walk in cooler with beer on tap. They agreed to trudge on.

Resourceful Charles had somehow materialized one of our two watermelons on the trip. We stopped at the barn he had located and had a nice cool watermelon before moving on. Ice had been in short supply during the whole trip. Recognizing that our ancestors probably didn't even know the luxury of ice at home, much less on the road, didn't stop our craving for it. I probably missed it the most. I like my cold drinks really cold. I want my glass to be so full of ice that the ice can't float. The thought of that full ice machine made those last few miles easier.

Charles Horchem and Janie Hull

Janie was on hand to greet us and announced that Morgan would cook for us. We met Morgan and his wife and son as we arrived. Royce arrived a short time later and welcomed the strangers that his wife had taken in as if it were an everyday occurrence. Royce was a large, handsome man with a welcoming smile and engaging manner. Quieter than Janie, but just as much fun. We were told to help ourselves to ice, beer on tap, and any other refreshments we wanted. The entire family was relaxed and totally hospitable.

As soon as the stock was taken care of, Janie took us to meet Bill Marquis, the owner of the log cabin we had visited before. Bill was standing beside the log cabin as we arrived. If we hadn't been travelling by automobile, everything and everybody looked like neighbors visiting neighbors one hundred and fifty years earlier. Bill looked completely at home with the log cabin. His hair, beard, clothing and demeanor said that he was reverent of history and comfortable in today's environment or one of a century and a half earlier. The cabin had been built in 1836 on a site several miles from where it stood today. Bill had torn it down piece by piece, including a stone fireplace and chimney, and reassembled it on his land in 1974. It was completely furnished with authentic period furniture, right down to eating and kitchen utensils.

As we exited the house, Janie urged him to tell us about the *Indian Vision*. He took us to the side of the house and asked us to look at the stones on the chimney outside. We gazed in awe at the level of craftsmanship it must have taken to take apart and reassemble each stone. We didn't see the real secret, however. Bill related a story about a visit from a Native American during the process of reassembling the house. This person had driven to the front of the house and walked purposefully up to gaze at the chimney. He had been driving along highway 380 and had been compelled to leave the road and come to this place he had never been before. He seemed very calm, thoughtful, and comfortable in approaching a strange house. Bill inquired as to his purpose. He smiled and said. "White men dream. Indians have visions. White men travel. Indians have vision quests. I had a vision as I passed this place on the main highway. I was guided to this place." Bill was interested, but understandably wary. He assumed the fellow was loco or had been drinking. However, when the man pointed to the chimney and said "There is the vision in the carving by my ancestors of the rock in this chimney; a prophecy of the future of the American Indian and the taking of their land and heritage by the white man." Bill looked up and could plainly see a wolf's head with a bone in its mouth and a bear claw. Though he had handled each stone many times and had numbered them so that they would be exactly right for reassembly, he had never seen the carvings in the stone before. With mouths open, we all quickly looked up to the spot he pointed to and could see the carvings clearly. I knew that this marked another memorable experience for this trail ride. I wanted to stay at this spot and study the carvings until sunset and possibly commune with my great grandmother's people. But it was not to be. Morgan was cooking, and Janie had invited guests to join us for the evening. I was relieved to hear that Bill and his wife would be attending. I wanted to hear more.

As we arrived back at camp, several neighbors had started to arrive for the impromptu party. Janie and Royce say that they will use any excuse to have a party and we provided the perfect one. I simply can't describe the meal we had that night. Suffice it to say that it included both beef and chicken fajitas, a few exotic dishes that I didn't recognize but that tasted wonderful, pie, brownies, cake and ice cream. Just as we were sitting down to eat, Jerald drove back in. He had been searching for quite a while, but finally spotted us in time to enjoy the terrific meal.

I visited more with Bill Marquis and his wife and discovered that she had been a photographer for the Centennial Wagon Train. Marion had a couple of mules that pulled a wagon for that entire journey. I also found out that Bill was in the *Guinness Book of World Records* for having the world's largest collection of barbed wire. He had accumulated over eleven thousand pieces from all over the world. His collection is in the Smithsonian now. He entertained us with stories of his world travel and adventures (some very dangerous) before he settled in little Stoney, Texas to live a simpler life.

Just as we finished our meal, Randy returned with son Tyler. Marion and I wanted to be sure that our grandchildren took part in this ride so they could tell their children and grandchildren about it. I momentarily wondered if the Hulls thought we had misled them about the number of guests, but they hardly seemed to notice our additions. Randy had killed a large rattler on the road up to the house and had it on display in the back of his truck. The neighbors showed only mild interest, but the rest of don't see rattlers that often in East Texas. I was not ready for the day to end, but fatigue was overtaking us. Even the young men were ready to bed down. Don't know if pulling those steer horns had anything to do with it or not.

Saturday, June 13

❦

Root Beer Pennington and Aubrey

The camp seemed much larger than it had been on our previous nights with the addition of Jerald, Randy, and Tyler and their two trucks. Charles was able to take the previous night off from cooking, so he prepared a good meal for us in the morning. The Hulls had coffee with us and discussed our route to reach Aubrey with the general consensus being that "you can't get there from here because you can't cross I-35". We had this discussion the previous evening and had been advised of several alternate routes to the one I had planned. They claimed them to be closer, more convenient, etc. . . . However, as the designated scout, I was stubborn during the entire trip about sticking to my map. Every time we had taken an alternate route, we had gotten lost. When you are traveling at about three miles per hour, you can't afford to get lost. I led the way to Krum, hoping I was right.

Marion had saddled Bonner for Tyler, thinking correctly that he could withstand the seven- year-old's light load. Tyler would have been about the same age as my dad on that original journey. Randy rode Jerald's palomino while Jerald rode the Buckskin. All horses were in use again for the first time since the second day of the trip. Joan and Don Stringer, along with my wife Jan, caught up with us just after lunch. Good to see my sweetheart after so long an absence. We both knew that I had many experiences during this trip not yet shared with her. It was something to savor and look forward to the telling. I realized they were there because it was a Saturday. For the first time since we left, I thought about the day of the week. I had brought along a pocket watch my kids had given me, but I had vowed not to look at it. I forgot to wind it most days.

As we entered Denton County, Jan, Joan and Don drove ahead to Krum for lunch, since we had already had our noon snack. When we reached Krum, I rode up to the restaurant on Rowdy. There was no place to "park" him, so I just looked through the window trying to see them. Finally, a waitress noticed me and came outside. She returned with Jan. I asked them to go down the road to see how we could get across Interstate 35. They followed the map and reported that we could not cross 35 at this juncture. I must have had some plan or seen something they hadn't when I made my scouting trip. Otherwise, I would not have put this route on my map. We headed on toward Aubrey. As we reached the interstate, I remembered what I had thought. We would go up the entry to the bridge the wrong way. Why shouldn't a covered wagon and a bunch of horses be able to do what cars can't? We posted folks at both ends and trudged up to the bridge. Jan

Left to right, Damon, Tyler and Bailey (mounted), Randy, Caden, Jim, and Jordan leaving Aubrey, Texas

Randy, Bailey, Tyler, Caden, and Jim. (Aubrey, Texas)

said that our crossing the interstate at three miles per hour while hundreds of cars raced under us at seventy and above was quite a sight. Another obstacle overcome. My confidence renewed, I led the way toward Aubrey.

Earlier that morning, Randy and I had taken his pickup and found a campsite at the home of Mr and Mrs. R. B. Pennington. Their home was at the intersection of two farm-to-market roads. She gave us permission to camp although RB was not at home. They had a large lot with many round hay bales stacked. More were coming in all the time. There was also a couple of barns and sheds as well as corrals for our stock. As we rode in, twins Jan and Joan were dutifully impressed with our "efficiency'" in setting up camp. We each had our routines established and knew what duties were to be done by each individual and which were to be shared. There was little confusion. Things just seem to happen when everyone takes his responsibility seriously. We never argued once over anything during the entire trip. The horses and mules were always fed and watered before we were. We all harangued Gordy mercilessly, but he was *in training* and that was to be expected. He took the ribbing like a man.

We made camp down by a small dry creek bed. It was warm again and fairly humid that day. The low spot we were in prevented breezes from reaching us. By this time the seasoned riders hardly noticed such small discomforts but our guests suffered a little. As we settled down for a good

meal of chicken fried steak, the Penningtons joined us for a short visit before heading into Aubrey. They told us of their three daughters living at
home and their history of the farm and ranch they operated. We discussed
the drought that was just beginning . They kindly and courageously offered
the use of their shower and bathroom while they were gone. I guess they
could tell we needed a little cleaning up. I told them I wanted their names
and addresses to send them a token of our appreciation. RB said to just remember Root Beer Pennington. Another fine hospitable family lives in
Texas.

Chiggers ran our visitors out of camp and back to Commerce as dark
approached. The young guys raced us older ones to see who could get into
that shower first. They won. First clean up in several days. Felt good.

Marion, Tyler, Caden, Bailey, and Jim in Aubrey, Texas

Sunday, June 14

❦

Grandchildren, Longhorns
and Buffalos

Pressing business had taken our cook away, possibly for the remainder of the trip. Randy and I took his truck and headed out early again to find our Sunday night campsite. As director of the Collin County Youth Park, Randy had frequent contact with Punk Carter, a well-known breeder and trainer of champion cutting horses. We visited his ranch and got permission to camp there from Shakes, an employee at the ranch. As we returned to meet the wagon, they were already a short distance from camp. The Pennington's young daughter had fulfilled a life long dream by riding Jerald's palomino into Aubrey beside the covered wagon. We were to send her many pictures of that event later.

As I approached the wagon, I noticed two especially beautiful young ladies seated on the wagon seat with Marion. I soon recognized granddaughters Bailey Kate Ainsworth (age four) and Peyton Macayla Boles (age four). I was delighted to see them. I knew that pictures would remind them of this ride throughout their lives. Parents Kevin and Shelly Boles, and Damon and Tia Ainsworth, along with my grandson Caden Kirk Ainsworth (age five) had gone down the road looking for me. They soon returned and joined us to ride through Aubrey. I took the reins to the mules so that Peyton and Bailey could ride with me while Marion rode my horse. The group had looked for us Saturday, but couldn't find us. They had spent the previous night in a motel close by.

We stopped just outside town to enjoy a snack and the cookies Shelly had baked for us. Caden rode beside me in the wagon while Bailey rode double with Tyler, the cousin she barely knew. It was definitely a special time for us. My family left about mid-afternoon as we continued our journey toward Celina, Collin County, and Punk Carter's ranch. The ride to the ranch was a scenic one. Having seen the place that morning, I knew we were in for a special evening. We found that Punk Carter was in Atlanta attending the American Cutting Horse Association convention. As Shakes led us past the main horse barn and corrals, the main house, and several outbuildings, we saw evidence that this was no ordinary ranch. Besides the nice cutting horse facilities, we saw longhorn cattle, buffalo, a guest house, a large lake, and a small very primitive cabin sitting alone on a hilltop.

We camped outside the guest house to be near corrals for our horses. Jerald helped us set up camp, took a few photos, and reluctantly left again for home. Back home, he was working on completing a barn and roping arena for me. He took Bonner for that much needed rest so that he could complete the final leg of the journey. Randy and Tyler also returned home so that only Marion, Gordy and I were left to enjoy this beautiful campsite.

Punk Carter Ranch Campsite.

Tack at rest—Punk Carter Ranch Lake

I don't remember the meal for that evening, but I am sure it wasn't hot and it wasn't up to Charles' standards. We took a cleansing swim in the lake and settled in for the evening.

Cooler weather and posting Gordy out of earshot allowed us to drift off early. About midnight, I heard a rustling beside my bed followed by a splashing sound. I awoke looking in the face of a curious longhorn steer about three inches from my nose. He was relieving himself beside my bed-roll. I looked over to see if Marion was observing this event, and saw a buffalo standing over his cot. Reaching for my camera scared the steer away, but I was able to get a shot of the buffalo. Gordy just kept snoring.

Next morning, Punk himself drove up to our campsite. Although we had been assured that he wouldn't mind our camping there, we were still a little embarrassed to be found on the property of a man we had never actually met. Our concerns were put to rest when he presented each of us with a bottle of privately labeled Punk Carter BBQ Sauce and welcomed us to his place. He told us that the place was frequently used for filming episodes of *Walker, Texas Ranger*, thus the need for the various buffalo and longhorns. As he led us out the easiest way, he noted that the cabin alone on the hilltop was built for filming *City Slickers*, but details were never worked out.

He was in very high spirits and informed us that he had been elected President of the ACHA the weekend before.

Marion leaving Punk Carter Ranch

Monday, June 15

❧~❧

Collin County Youth Barn and Farm Museum and Blue Ridge

Marion, Gordy, and I left Punk's place heading for Melissa and Blue Ridge. Randy had given us instructions on how to reach Collin County Youth Barn and Farm Museum where he works. We stopped at the beautiful location and had a light snack in impressive surroundings. We visited the old jail on the property and were interviewed by a McKinney newspaper. We reluctantly left this picturesque spot to go on to Melissa.

Randy caught up with us again in Melissa around lunchtime. He brought us some fried chicken to eat by the side of the road. I think everyone thought that Marion and I would starve if left to our own resources. As we headed past Melissa, we rode on one of the first dirt roads of the whole trip. We had seen lots of gravel, oil, rock and other types of roads, but this one was a county road that ran through a field of milo and other row crops. It looked as if it had never seen the blade of a maintainer. It was smooth, but the thing that impressed us most was the quiet. The wagon made no sound. On hard surfaces, it groaned, popped and rattled. Another significant difference between this trip and the first one. Daddy's family must have enjoyed listening only to the sound of hooves on soft dirt and birds singing.

Marion and I both recalled working hours in fields like this pulling bolls. We would ride home on the fenders of old cars down soft country roads after a hard day in the cotton patch. If we passed Ward's store at Klondike or

Mill's Camp Lake store at Shiloh, we might stop for a big Baby Ruth and a coke.

When we reached Blue Ridge, we knew that we had no prearranged place to stay and no vehicles to search for us. As we entered the town just before dusk, we turned to see Jerald behind us. He was a welcome sight. Jan, also thinking we would starve, had sent him with beans, cornbread, and iced tea. Bless her heart, we would have a hot meal tonight. We camped beside the Blue Ridge Riding Club arena and enjoyed Jan's cooking. When we unsaddled, Marion discovered a new hole in his saddle bag. He had lost his camera. That left only my photos of us crossing the Brazos. Duty called Jerald back home and we settled into camp for this eleventh night away from home.

Tuesday, June 16

❦

A Bridge not to Cross
and Hanging at Scatterbranch

In the absence of our cocinero, we left Blue Ridge early after a cold breakfast. We soon entered Hunt County. It seemed incredible that we were already in my home county but still two days away from the end of our journey. We stopped in Celeste, a small town, and watered the stock from a hose at a convenience store. Strange as it may seem, I was more concerned about this leg of the trip because it had been dark and muddy the night I scouted it. I couldn't travel all of the roads due to mud and trees that had blown down during a storm. As we headed out of Celeste, Jan arrived again bringing last granddaughter Taylor Nabers (age three). Little Brother Landon was only a little over one, so he was not quite old enough to make it. Taylor was wearing a little railroad cap that had belonged to her father. When she took her seat beside me on the wagon, she said, "I heard you wanted me to come see you." She was right. I wanted all the grandchildren who were old enough to participate in the trip.

About an hour after Taylor joined me, we approached our first questionable bridge. It was made of steel mesh with no side rails. I could see that Clyde was a little skittish as we approached, but I was not worried. They had seen much more frightening things during this trip and never faltered. He balked when we approached the edge. I handed Taylor down to Gordy, who took her across the bridge and sat her on his horse. As we were doing this, two young girls came along to watch the spectacle. I climbed back into the wagon and put the reins to the mules. Bell wanted to cross, but Clyde would not. I didn't realize it, but Gordy had come back across the bridge, leaving his horse (and Taylor) in the care of the two girls. The mules struggling against each other and the reins caused Gordy's horse to act up and the little girls holding it simply dropped the reins and started to scream. This frightened Taylor. She didn't cry, but she was understandably upset. I got down from the wagon, calmed her, set her on Rowdy (whom she loves) and handed the reins to Gordy with the admonition to not let them out of his hands.

Back to the mules. Marion and I realized that Clyde could possibly go over the side and take everything connected to him along. That included Bell, the wagon, and me. We decided that it wasn't worth the risk. We would have to find an alternate route. As we started to back up and turn around, Joe Bob Shaffer arrived with son Hadley and a big trailer with Hadley's horse inside. We unharnessed the mules, put them in the trailer, pulled the wagon across, pulled the mules across in the trailer and hitched them back to the wagon. Lost time—about thirty minutes. Time saved—about half a

Taylor Nabers and Jim

day. Hadley, the son of Marion's sister Kathy Shaffer, had come along to ride the rest of the way with us. His arrival was perfect timing. More good luck? Just as we crossed the bridge, we were surprised to see Charles coming from behind. We had not expected to see him again before the final day of the trip. He had followed our wagon tracks to find us and made fun of their meandering path. I assured him that his path was just as wandering when he had been driving.

About mid afternoon, Jan joined us again and took me to look at a couple of places she had found for us to camp overnight. It seemed strange to be in her car again. I felt a little claustrophobic after being outside continuously for so long. We stopped at Betty Myers' Little Creek Ranch in Scatterbranch, a small community outside Commerce, and she extended her welcome to spend the night. Her house is over 100 years old and sits near a spot noted for a hanging that occurred before the turn of the twentieth century. The ranch has passed down through three generations. Her father-in-law first showed her a very old tree with a huge limb reaching out over the creek. As the story has been passed down for generations, a man was hanged there and his body left swinging over the creek as a lesson for cattle rustlers.

As we drove through our own home county, I began to realize that we were close to the end of our journey. The realization sort of shocked me. I had immersed myself in daily thoughts of our planned journey and reliving things that my ancestors had experienced. There was little thought of completion, just continuing. I was surprised to feel a strong sense of pride and accomplishment at that point. We were almost home. When I rejoined the others, Pal O'Nina was the horse that was most available so I rode him the rest of the way.

We pulled into Ms. Myers' home well before sundown, watered the stock in her nearby pool, then sat down to prematurely pat ourselves on the back. She brought us lots of cold water (with plenty of ice). It seemed strange to be camping this close to home. I was only fifteen minutes by car from my home and only five hours away horseback. Yet, our journey was not complete. We planned to camp at the same site that our forebears had in Shiloh, Dogtown Road, Delta County, Texas.

As we unsaddled the horses for camp that night, I thought about how easy and routine it had become to saddle and unsaddle, water, groom and feed a horse that is your only means of transportation. When I used to ride only occasionally, it became a nuisance and downright hard to sling a saddle over a horse's back. Now, even with a slicker and full saddlebags added, it had become easy.

Before we could get supper ready, we were joined by lots of friends and relatives. Ms. Myers' family visited with us, also. Jerald returned with Bonner. He also brought along his dad, Pop Thomas. Rick Vanderpool returned to interview us for the *Commerce Journal*, Laurie White King was there for the *Greenville Herald Banner*, and Lori Cope for *Country World*. Not having seen a newspaper for two weeks, we were surprised at the interest in our trail ride. Local newspapers had picked it up as a Fathers Day special feature since the ride had been to honor our fathers. With everyone gathered around, this was definitely the climax of the trip for me. Not when I expected it to happen, but happen it did. I felt we were at home, though we had not reached our destination. I sort of expected revelry from our little group of travelers, but I noticed that we all seemed simply and quietly content.

Jim and Rowdy

Wednesday, June 17

Downtown Commerce
and Shiloh

As we saddled up to ride into Commerce, we again had the newspapers there to chronicle this last leg of the trip. Rob Stanley of KETR radio was also present. Just as he asked me questions about my horse, Rowdy nickered loudly into the microphone. Months later, Quentin Morris, an uncle I had not seen in years, told me he had heard that broadcast. When we started, a few scattered raindrops fell, but not enough to get anything wet. By the time we reached town, it had cleared to a beautiful day.

Judging from the many pictures taken that morning on our way to Commerce, I sat my horse in a physical slump indicating a tiredness that I did not feel yet. Besides our basic group, Jerald had rejoined us and Hadley remained with us to make five riders. Marion was back on Bonner. Someone later asked me ask why it was important to him to ride Bonner on the last leg of the trip. I replied, "If you have to ask, you wouldn't understand." Charles drove the mules with both flags flying from the wagon. As we headed down the familiar Live Oak Street toward the square, we saw cousin Kent Humphries leaning against his pickup and watching our small parade. Kent's mother Exle had been on that original journey.

We turned north on Washington and were looking at dowtown Commerce. As we crossed Sycamore, I could see wife Jan, daughter Shelly, and granddaughters Peyton and Taylor. That brought warmth to my tired bones. We entered the square, turned ease on main and came back to the

Taylor Nabers, Jim Ainsworth, and Peyton Boles in downtown Commerce.

vacant lot beside Jerald's world famous Cowhill Express Coffee Shop. Jerald and wife Elaine treated us all to frozen cappuccino. Jerald's daughter, Wendy Ellyson with husband Clint and daughters Chaney and Mackenzie, were also there to greet us. We rode our horses on the sidewalk and up to the door of the coffee shop to give our grandchildren a hug and a ride.

We enjoyed our refreshments until Charles lay down on the grass for a nap. It was then that we decided it was time to head for Shiloh. Mackenzie and Peyton rode in the wagon with Charles, and Chaney rode with her grandfather aboard Pal O'Nina. She was asleep on his shoulder within an hour of our departure. After only a short distance in the wagon, Taylor remembered the incident with the mules on the bridge and elected to stay with her Gran Jan. As we headed down Bonham Alley toward Park Street and out of town, I noticed Geronimo's shoes again. They were past clicking and into loud popping. You could literally see them move with each step. Marion and I had lost our bet, though. Not a single shoe fell off—and the horse lived through three colic episodes. He was three hundred pounds lighter, but still alive.

Charles Horchem, Clyde and Blue—downtown Commerce

Jordan, Mackenzie, Jerald, Chaney, Jim, Hadley, Charles, and Marion at Delta County line

Jan and Shelly met us just after we crossed into Delta County, our seventh and final Texas county. They brought sandwich fixins' and cold drinks. We ate close to Horton community on a dirt road. As we neared Shiloh community, Marion rode ahead to Shiloh Cemetery. He reined his horse to a stop in front of Arch's grave, removed his hat, and paid silent homage to his departed father.

Hildred Shaw, Marion's mother, was waiting for us at Kathy Shaffer's house. She rode in the wagon the rest of the way to her home on Dogtown Road. She lives at the site where our parents and grandparents first camped at the end of their journey. Both Marion and I had lived on Dogtown Road at some time in our lives. My father and mother, Teadon and Nadelle, built a home not over half a mile from the campsite. Arch and Hildred lived at the site. Our parents had pointed out an old oak tree many times as the site of their original camp. That tree died a few years ago. When it was cut down, Marion retrieved a limb with a horseshoe grown into it. From the rings on the tree, it appears to have been there about eighty years. We like to think it came from one of the horses that brought our parents here. As we set up our final camp, we took pictures at the stump that remains from that giant oak tree. We had achieved our objective.

Later that night, we were joined again by friends, neighbors and relatives for a celebration. Justin Nabers brought daughter Taylor out. Marion's sisters Kathy Shaffer and Kay Moore joined us and also families and friends of the other riders. We enjoyed Jan's, Pat's and Trish's excellent home made ice cream and the other food that our families and friends had brought. No cooking for Charles tonight. Taylor and Whitney Lajaunie, both three, repeated many games that we had played two generations earlier. I was reminded of simpler times when Arch and Teadon's families gathered outside in the summer to visit and share ice cream or watermelon. They would have been pleased to see our gathering that evening.

Marion at Arch's Grave—Shiloh Cemetery, Delta County, Texas

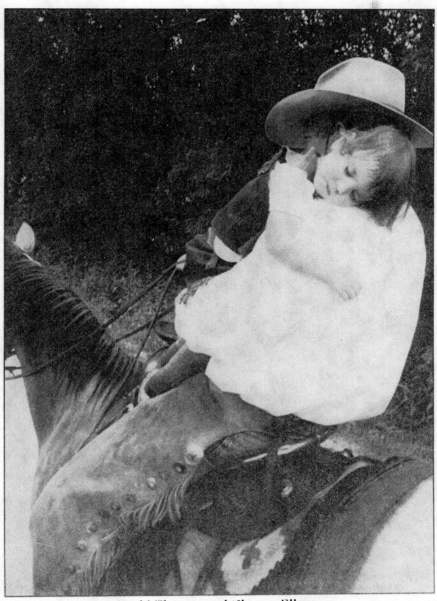

Jerald Thomas and Chaney Ellyson

Jordan, Jim, Hadley, Tyler and Marion at the Shiloh oak tree stump.

Thursday, June 18

❦

West Delta, Klondike and Cooper Images from the Past

We didn't sleep well our last night to camp out. Maybe it was the strong wind, possibly the ants, but I think it was because we were too close to our own beds. Although we had reached our original destination, we had agreed to finish the journey on the Cooper Square. Marion had taken a lot of ribbing from his coffee shop buddies about not finishing the trip. He had promised to ride his horse up to their table in the coffee shop. We intended to provide any verification that he needed.

As we prepared to head for Cooper, Charles sent a message to Jack Anderson, an elderly black gentleman that had a long association with Charles and his family. He wanted him to ride on the wagon during this last day. Jack was enthusiastic and said he would start to meet us right away. Knowing he did not own a car, Charles asked how he was going to get there. He replied simply "I'll start walking right now." Charles arranged for someone to bring him to us on Highway 24. As we headed out on our last leg of the journey, the original group was joined by Jerald, Hadley, and Tyler.

As we neared the community of West Delta, the fatigue I had been denying started taking over. My mind and my eyes were drifting. As we passed the road to the place where I had spent the first fourteen years of my life, I could clearly see a boy about nine or ten dressed in a red and white baseball uniform, a red cap with a big letter D on it. He was standing at the entrance to the lane where I had lived but was looking down Highway 24. His thumb was set in a definite hitchhiking plea. I had hitched many rides to games and practices when I played in the initial year of Delta County Little League Baseball. Practices and games were six miles away in Cooper and I never missed either. If my parents were at work, I bummed a ride. Nobody could pass up a boy in a baseball cap. If I had on my uniform, the first car always stopped. If I wore only the cap, it might take two or three before I caught a ride. I wished that my children or my grandchildren could feel safe in doing that today.

A quarter mile further down the road, I could almost see the site where Papa Hiram's small house stood deep in the pasture where we had lived. Daddy and Arch had built it for him after Eva's death. It was a simple house with only three rooms. It sort of resembled a present day A-frame cabin with a small porch. As I let my mind drift, I remembered riding my horse through our back pasture to his front door. I usually carried a gallon of fresh milk from our milk cow or a few eggs. I remember insisting on riding to Papa's, even when I was carrying milk in a gallon glass jug. Mother was afraid I would spill it, so Daddy made a leather handle that allowed me to hold it and ride bareback. If I didn't ride old Scar, Papa would admonish, "You need to ride that horse every day, Bolivar." I never questioned why he called me Bolivar.

He continued to ride his horse, old Buddy, until he was in his late seventies. When his daughters insisted that he stop riding "that old Bronc" he replaced the horse with a motorcycle. When I brought him milk or eggs, he usually pressed a few "coppers," his word for pennies, in my palm. I had been told to steadfastly refuse them, but he would usually hold me while he dropped them in my pocket. If we both had time on our hands, or if it "commenced" to rain, I could usually beg a little fiddle music.

His bachelor life always interested me. I loved to look at his simple eating and cooking utensils. He lived much the same way as his father had. No running water, no inside bathroom, no heating or cooling. He ate with forks and knives that had yellow bone handles that I thought were beautiful. The aroma of bacon and black coffee always permeated the house. When I asked him who cooked for him or sewed his buttons, he told me of the little woman who stayed in his attic. I wanted to see her, but not bad enough to crawl through the small hole that led to the attic. Eva Catherine died in 1939 and Papa remained a bachelor for twenty three years until his death in 1962.

Only a quarter mile further, we passed the old site of West Delta School. I had spent my first eight years of school there, and Marion had graduated there. When West Delta consolidated with Cooper, the old building was turned into a hospital. Charles had been its first chef, even though he was still a teenager. The hospital was later converted to apartments. It gradually

deteriorated and was torn down only a year before our trip. The old buildings from the past were very visible to three riders that day, however.

As we neared Klondike, memories of Ward's store and Dad Moore's
store filled my head. Daddy used to go to Dad Moore's store to spit and
whittle on a rainy morning. I would play outside or drink a coke with the
men. Dad's was once the subject of an article on small town general stores
in the *Dallas Morning News*. Pictures were taken of the dirt dauber nests
in the twenty dollar bill slot in Dad's cash register. Ward's store was out on
highway 24 and was often the pickup point for baseball games since Harry
Ward was my baseball coach. Someone would drop me off there and I would
ride to practice or games with Harry in the back of his pickup. I remember
my parents charging groceries there when times were tough. Once a stop
for the railroads and home to two banks and several stores, Klondike has
dwindled to only a few residents and no stores.

Jack Anderson arrived somewhere around Klondike. Dressed in overalls and a cap and chewing on a cigar, he had that ageless look we attributed
to Oaks Crossing Slim. He displayed agility as he boarded the wagon and
took his seat beside Charles. Without a word, Charles handed him the
reins. He put them in hands that had obviously held reins before. With a
gentle cluck to the mules, we were on our way. I couldn't help but be reminded of the words to Tom T. Hall's song that refers to an old *gray black
gentleman*. The fellow sits down uninvited by Tom and starts to give him
his philosophy on life that goes something like *There ain't nuthin' in this
old world wuth a solitary dime, 'cept old dogs and children, and watermelon wine.* I hummed that song in my head until we reached Cooper. I
idly wondered about his other song that included a philosopher who said
the secret of life was *faster horses, younger women, older whiskey, and
more money.* Were they contradictory?

My mind also wandered to the many western movies I had seen at
Sparks Theater in Cooper, or at the Bloody Bucket and Palace Theater in
Commerce. These heroes of the silver screen took off on longer journeys
than ours with nothing but saddlebags. Next morning, they drank coffee
from a cup poured from a coffeepot and ate their breakfast from a skillet.
Where did those things come from? Would Marion and I have been able to
make the trip without the wagon? It was satisfying that we had made the
entire trip without serious injury to man or beast. Not a horse or mule had
even lost a shoe.

As Marion led us past the Cooper city limits sign, I took one last look at
our group. It was tired, but contented. Newspapers would later mention our
cowboy tans and "faces etched by years in the sun", etc. I looked down and
saw daddy's rusted and wrinkled hands holding my reins. We stopped at

Jack Anderson and Charles Horchem on the road to Cooper.

Marions Car Care Center while he hassled his employees to work harder. Then on to the restaurant where pooled bets had been taken as to how long Marion would last. He rode up to the entrance to claim his winnings. We stopped at the Patterson Delta County Museum in the old Cooper train depot and posed for snapshots. That old building was built in 1913, five years before Papa came here. We think he rode those tracks. We stopped again on the downtown square for pictures at the pagoda. Jerald had delivered my trailer to the square, so we headed toward it to load for home. Max Moody, Delta County Commissioner and master farrier, was pleased to see his handiwork still firmly in place as he helped us load. We headed back to Commerce and home. Marion, Charles, Gordy, and Hadley completed the few miles remaining to reach Marion's house. Our journey was complete.

At home, wife Jan had made a quilt to commemorate our journey. She had symbols for the original journey in 1918, our 1998 journey, our grandfather and grandmother, the five siblings, Teadon and Arch, and Marion and

I. She had artfully summarized everything into a beautiful quilt that I now proudly display. I am sure that its meaning and value will continue to increase each year for the rest of our lives. As I carefully examined it to understand each of her symbols, I thought about the results of that original journey. Of the original travellers, only one remains. Exle is in failing health and was only two in 1918. There is nobody left who remembers that wagon trip. What happened to that original family? What was the dramatic impact of moving from West Texas to East Texas?

Mabel married and lived most of her adult years as a homemaker in Ft.Worth (where the West begins). Husband Paul Nelson worked primarily as a draftsman for construction companies. Ola married George Allison and they lived most of their adult lives in Dallas. Ola was a homemaker and George worked in construction related businesses, also. Arch and Hildred raised three children while working primarily in farming and ranching near that original campsite. Until his death, Arch continued to trade horses and tell stories about horses Papa Hiram or he had owned. Teadon and Nadelle also raised three children. Teadon was a jack of all trades. He worked as a

Delta County Museum in Cooper, Texas

heavy equipment operator, mechanic, electrician, carpenter, farmer and rancher. He returned to West Texas for a couple of years to farm, but Northeast Texas had become his true home. When he died, he lived less than a mile from that original campsite.

Laurie White King wrote of us in the *Greenville Herald Banner,*

Riding with the easy grace of people born to the saddle, they loomed as large as any of the characters in a Larry McMurtry novel. Leading the outfit astride a stout sorrel gelding was Jim Ainsworth, face etched by years in the sun, trail boss and scout of this one wagon train. Following, but apart was Ainsworth's trusty sidekick and true cousin, weathered, garulous Marion Ainsworth.

Behind them came the muleskinner Charles Horchem, perched high on his wagon seat flanked on either side by the Texas and American Flags, cursing and caressing his team with a firm, gravelly voice. And pulling up the rear, the youth of this crew, sixteen-year-old Jordan Brown, lounged comfortably back in his saddle, more at home with his horse Geronimo than most people.

Hiram and Eva Ainsworth's Children—Teadon, Mabel, Exle, Hiram, Ola, and Arch

We enjoyed Laurie's description, but realize that what we did was of little note on a global or world scale. We didn't even mention the trip to many people when we were planning it. Many who heard about it simply asked "Why?" Once we had completed the trip, many probably asked "So what?" I can't explain it. I do know this. If one grandchild hears about the trip or sees a photo taken during the trip; if one says, "Look what Papa did;" if one of my compadres of the trip greets me with a bellowing *Braaaaazoos* that speaks volumes of good memories; if one person who reads this chronicle says, "I wish I had been there", then it was worth it. Life is made up of memories, experiences and relationships. Some happy, some sad, some good, some bad. This goes in the good and happy columns. What a man has experienced, no power on earth can take away.

About the Trail Riders . . .

Several people participated and assisted in this journey, but these are the major participants.

Tommy Chalaire is a coach and teacher in Lamar County, Texas. Randy Lajaunie continues to manage the Collin County Youth Barn and Farm Museum. Jerald Thomas owns and operates Jeta Construction Co. and Cowhill Express Coffee Co. in Commerce, Texas and runs two major concessions at First Monday Trade Days in Canton, Texas. His products are distributed nationwide and he is famous for being the man *brave enough to sell Cappuccino in Texas*. Jordan Brown continues his athletic and academic pursuits in Highland Park, Dallas and still spends time with friend and mentor, Charles Horchem. Charles is an entrepreneur who has worked in financing, sales and marketing of mobile homes. He has also dabbled in fence and building construction, registered cattle, insurance, storage buildings, and real estate development. He lives on a ranch in Winnsboro, Texas. Marion Ainsworth, also an entrepreneur, has had a dairy, managed a feed and grain company, raised cattle, and now owns Car Care Center in Cooper, Texas. He spent his entire life living at or near the site of that first camp on Dogtown Road. He now lives outside Cooper and continues to keep a horse and a few cows. Jim Ainsworth, the author, while spending most of his life in Northeast Texas, lived for three years in the Texas Panhandle during his youth. That pivotal period deepened his interest in all things Texan and in western history. Living eight years in large cities early in his career convinced him that rural life was better. Like his trail companions, he is an entrepreneur. Starting with a retail store specializing in Western Wear and Tack, he simultaneously opened a small Certified Public Accounting practice in Commerce, Hunt County, Texas. He later added a Certified Financial Planning practice and investment management firm. He subsequently co-founded a full service financial services firm including a broker-dealer. He has written and had published three books related to the financial services industry. In 1997, he sold all his business interests, built a barn and roping arena, and started to team rope. He is a regular participant and frequent loser in team roping events.

Index

LaVergne, TN USA
14 January 2010
169944LV00004B/20/P